n+1
udp

n+1 / ugly duckling presse
eastern european poets series #30
second edition, 2016

Kirill Medvedev
It's No Good

Edited and introduced by Keith Gessen

Translated from the Russian by Keith Gessen with
Mark Krotov, Cory Merrill, and Bela Shayevich

It's No Good: poems / essays / actions
Copyright denied by Kirill Medvedev, 2012, 2016

Translations copyright 2012, 2016
by Keith Gessen, Mark Krotov, Cory Merrill, Bela Shayevich

Eastern European Poets Series #30
Series Editor: Matvei Yankelevich
Guest Translations Editor: Isabel Lane

Second Edition, 2016
First Edition, 2012

ISBN 978-1-937027-82-7

n+1, 68 Jay Street #405, Brooklyn, NY 11201
Ugly Duckling Presse, 232 Third Street #E303, Brooklyn, NY 11215

Distributed to the trade by Small Press Distribution
(spdbooks.org)

Available directly from the publishers
(nplusonemag.com; uglyducklingpresse.org)

///

The translation of this book was partially funded by a grant
from the New York State Council on the Arts, a state agency.

The book was made possible in part by a generous grant
from the National Endowment for the Arts.

Portions of this book have appeared in *Aufgabe*, *Dissent*, and *n+1*.

///

Design by Don't Look Now!
Typeset in Adobe Garamond, with titles in Univers
Printed in the USA by McNaughton & Gunn
Covers printed offset by Prestige Printing

Kirill Medvedev
It's No Good
poems / essays / actions

TABLE OF CONTENTS

It's No Good

KIRILL MEDVEDEV: AN INTRODUCTION

I first learned of Kirill Medvedev in Fall 2006, when someone handed me a copy of the literary magazine *Kriticheskaya Massa* ("Critical Mass," now defunct), featuring a symposium about the release of Medvedev's book by the Novoe Literaturnoe Obozrenie (NLO) publishing house. The book's release required a symposium because Medvedev had renounced all copyright to his works, and NLO had nonetheless gone ahead and published the book without asking his permission. They called it *Texts Published Without the Permission of the Author*. One essay defended the publication; another, "The Surrender and Death of a Post-Soviet Intellectual"—by the poet, editor, and impresario Dmitry Kuzmin—attacked the author. There was also an essay by Medvedev himself, reprinted (again without permission) from his website. The day after reading all this I found the book in question at the annual Moscow Book Fair. I read it on the subway ride home. It was a mixture of poems and essays and descriptions of Medvedev's (often one-man) political actions. I couldn't believe what I was reading. After failing to find another copy of the book at several stores, I finally located three at Falanster, off Tverskaya, and bought them all.

How to describe the political and cultural and just plain human stagnation of the years of mature Putinism, between about 2003 and 2008? "Fear" is not the right word. Moscow has always been a dangerous place, but it was no scarier in 2006 than it was in 1996—it was a lot less scary, in fact. Putin himself, ruler of Russia, was certainly a bad man. But he was not the bogeyman. The atmosphere was of boredom, suffocation, and surrender. Nothing happened. No one wanted anything to happen. "Stability" was the word of the day and in service of this stability people were willing to give up a great deal. The liberal opposition that still made appearances in the *New York Times* not only had no real presence in Russia—no party organization, no television stations, no support—they were also thoroughly discredited. They had taken power in the post-Soviet period on a wave of popular anger and hope and had disappointed those hopes; they had proved vain, callow, visibly indifferent to the sufferings of millions. (These people unfortunately included many urban intellectuals, formerly known as the intelligentsia. They hated the Soviet Union so much, were so happy to see it gone, that they refused to see how bad things were getting until it was too late.) By late 2003, after the arrest of the oligarch Mikhail Khodorkovsky signaled the final end of the hopes of the 1990s, political opposition to Putin came to consist on the one hand of a weird party of teenage outcasts, part Stalinist, part anarchist, led by a former poet turned revolutionary turned federal prisoner named Eduard Limonov (he served a two-year sentence beginning in 2001 for illegal purchase of firearms), and on the other of Chechen terrorists. Real power was wielded by a cabal of businessmen and politicians and businessmen-turned-politicians (and vice versa). Occasionally for prying into business transactions—but not for any political speech or position—a journalist would get shot.

All this, plus money. Russia is a huge exporter of oil, natural gas, nickel, and aluminum. Between 1998 and 2008, prices for these and other raw materials rose, in some instances, by an order of magnitude. The country was awash in cash. And so in addition to total political and cultural stagnation, a culture of "luxury" sprang up; people were buying luxury cars and suits and thousand-Euro leather jackets. In response, a great many people threw in the towel. It was almost impossible to participate in politics; the remaining cultural institutions were either irrelevant, cowed, or (in the case of the new glossy consumer magazines, like Russian *Esquire*) entirely geared toward the nascent bourgeoisie; it was better to get what you could while the getting was good.

This was the cultural, political, and social situation in the fall of 2006, when I found Medvedev's book. The crusading journalist Anna Politkovskaya had just been shot in her elevator, and Putin had as much as spit on her grave a few days later. To the great indignation of the international press, he declared that no one in Russia cared about Politkovskaya—*and he was right*. She was shot and it didn't matter. Perhaps it was time to pack it in for the next decade or so.

The author of *Texts Published Without...* was just 31 years old. He had published, through traditional channels, one book of poetry—*Vsyo plokho* ("Everything's Bad," or "It's No Good")—and another book, *Vtorzhenie* ("Incursion"), that was a mixture of poetry and essays. Both had been well-received by critics, although also denounced in some circles as self-indulgent, "not poetry," and so on. The poems were free verse, which put them slightly outside the Russian poetic tradition; they were more reminiscent of Charles Bukowski (whom Medvedev had translated) than any Russian predecessor. But what put them really outside the Russian tradition was their everyday-ness. It was bad enough for a poet not to rhyme, but to discuss at length how he found some cheap pâté at an expensive supermarket—and not as a metaphor for anything, really: he was mostly pleased to have found some cheap pâté—was a little much, or too little. There had been a strain of anti-Romantic Russian poetry going back all the way to Pushkin; in the late Soviet period, especially, the great conceptualist poets, Dmitri Prigov chief among them, enjoyed puncturing the pretensions of highly rhetorical Soviet poetry with their verse-tales of going to the store to buy stale bread. (The Soviet conceptualist novel par excellence was Vladimir Sorokin's *The Queue* (1984), the entirety of which took place in a line outside a store.) So it wasn't as if Russian poetry had never not rhymed, and it wasn't as if it had never been to the supermarket. The difference may have been that Medvedev, while doing away with much of the formal apparatus of Russian lyric poetry, had retained its messianic element. He was not an ironist; he was very much a Poet. In the end, as Medvedev says of his one-time friend turned antagonist Dmitry Kuzmin, the combination of all these things in one person proved really very aggravating.

Medvedev's evolution as a poet and thinker leading up to his renunciation of copyright and rejection of the literary world was visible in his first two books. The poems in his first book, *It's No Good*, were memoiristic and introspective, though that book, too, began with a rejection—of translation. The first poem of

Medvedev's first book declared that he would no longer translate other poets, but be himself a poet. The rest of the book expanded, confidently and sometimes exuberantly, on this discovery. In his second book, *Incursion*, doubt began to creep in: poems and essays responded to his critics, made further declarations, pleaded for more time. The book included a long essay on the terrorist attacks of September 11; a discussion of Medvedev's translations of American pornographic novels; and some reflections on the different Russian words for cock and cunt. It concluded with a long diary about the author's frustrations with money and publishing and writing that was framed as annotations to the published diary of the dean of the Gorky Literary Institute.

Then came the break with the literary world. Looking back on it, Medvedev has said that what troubled him most about the reception of his first two books was not the criticism of his poetry, nor, on the other hand, that some people really liked his poetry and were willing to publish more of it—but that, in the end, all of this was in some profound way irrelevant. Arguments about poetry never spilled over into real life. They did not change anyone's behavior. They certainly (this was in 2002, 2003) did not affect anyone's view of whether the United States should invade Iraq.

Medvedev began, by his own account, to read more deeply and widely, especially in leftist political philosophy. He concluded that he must change his life. On his website he announced that he would no longer participate in the literary scene in any of its manifestations: no publications, no readings, and in fact he no longer claimed any copyright to his work. Only pirated editions: no contracts. He began writing long essays, which he posted online, about the fate of the Russian intelligentsia. And eventually he took to the streets. In early 2007, a few months after I discovered his book and started giving it out to my friends, my sister, a journalist in Moscow, sent me a link to a Russian news story. "Is this your Medvedev?" she asked. The article described how Medvedev had set up a one-man protest in front of a fashionable theater in central Moscow because the director had signed a letter in support of

Putin but was now staging a play by the anti-totalitarian poet and playwright Bertolt Brecht. One of the theater's guards came out, infuriated, and punched Medvedev, who nonetheless continued his protest. That was my Medvedev, all right.

As I read Medvedev's critique of the Moscow literary and intellectual world, what struck me above all was how it answered so many of the questions my friends and I had been struggling with in New York. Here we were, writing about the depredations of multinational corporations—how they dodged taxes, off-shored work to places with lax or no labor laws, and destroyed the environment—and then publishing our books or articles with places that were owned by ... multinational corporations. But it was complicated. Viking-Penguin, which published my first book, was owned by the large British company Pearson, which made its money selling books and educational software. In the past Viking-Penguin had published writers like Saul Bellow and Don DeLillo; on the other hand, in 1990, it declined to publish the paperback version of Salman Rushdie's *Satanic Verses* after the Iranian fatwa, in a craven surrender to intimidation and censorship. Still, Viking-Penguin is hardly Exxon-Mobil. On the other hand HarperCollins, with which I'd also published a book, is owned by Rupert Murdoch's right-wing media empire, NewsCorp—a lot more like Exxon-Mobil. On the third hand, Harper is the only major New York publisher whose employees have formed a union. And on the fourth hand...

Medvedev cut through all this. In the Russia of the 1990s and early '00s, the blood of the oligarchs was still visibly on their hands. Those hands were not meant for shaking. Sure, it was complicated—nice, well-meaning people worked at those publishing houses, magazines, etc., and one always needed the money—but it wasn't *that* complicated. Medvedev likes to quote Brecht on writers who "imagine that they have got hold of an apparatus which in fact has got hold of them." To play within the system is to play by its rules; you could choose, also, to walk away, and that's what Medvedev did.

There was more. In his essays on the intelligentsia—"My Fascism," "Dmitry Kuzmin," "Literature Will Be Tested"— Medvedev began to unravel the problems that had bedeviled us in the US for years. What is the proper relationship of literature to politics? Isn't the writer's job simply to write good books and then get them out to as wide an audience as possible? And what, exactly, is wrong with the playful omnivorousness that characterized much of what came to be associated with youth or "hipster" culture in the late '90s and early '00s? Isn't it good to mix and match, to swallow other styles and assimilate them to your own?

Medvedev's answers to these questions are consistent. In his long, careful essay on Kuzmin, Medvedev describes the construction of a post-ideological literary empire—at a certain point serving a progressive function, opening up space for new writing, but eventually ossifying into reaction, sentimentalism, and defensiveness, because at a certain point it is not simply enough to "publish good writing." In "Literature Will Be Tested," Medvedev describes another tendency in contemporary literature—the hunger for "authentic," personal expression, after the postmodernist refusal of it, and how this, too, can turn rancid if it is not consciously and consistently thought through and critiqued. What is an author for? asks Medvedev. Is he a private citizen who tries to produce masterpieces of literature—whereupon his responsibilities end? The answer, especially in contemporary Russia, must be *no*. The author must be willing to answer for his texts. The only justification for an essentially unproductive life is that it be lived without compromise.

Medvedev's critique of the "personal project," of the author seeking to separate public art and "private life," contemporary vanity and eternal artistic glory, is primarily directed at liberal authors and critics, followers of Joseph Brodsky, who, despite being humane and sympathetic themselves, ultimately serve to legitimize the much less humane project of atomization and depoliticization. But Medvedev also identifies another tendency in contemporary Russian culture, one that is very adept at connecting art to life and politics and the present day; that rejects material concerns; that is infused with the fire and force of self-sacrifice, God, and nation. This tendency is fascism, and it is very much alive. Of course contemporary fascism will not always look like fascism from the 1930s (though, as Medvedev points out, it looks close enough). It can manifest itself as a paranoid obsession with "the West"; or with Chechens; or with Fifth Column liberals. In the "Eurasian" project of Alexander Dugin, Russian fascism even does away with the master race. Medvedev is certainly not the first person to point out that Dugin (and his one-time partner, Eduard Limonov) has been flirting with fascism. The difference is that Medvedev diagnoses the attractiveness of what they're offering. The far right has solved something that needed solving, and done so in a powerful way: they have connected politics and art. The enemies of fascism must do the same.

///

Medvedev's final contribution is the beginning of a solution. Highly critical of the post-Soviet liberal intelligentsia, he is none-theless one of the only contemporary Russian writers who has fully acknowledged the scope of its tragedy. These wonderful, erudite, sensitive people of our parents' generation, the liberal intelligentsia, the friends of Brodsky, the fans of Vladimir Vysotsky—what happened to them? Why did they so badly mangle their historic opportunity? (Medvedev's own father, Felix Medvedev, whom he mentions in these pages, was a popular journalist during the perestroika era. In 1987, amid a media blackout, he courageously announced at the Soviet Union of Writers in Moscow that Brodsky had won the Nobel Prize. According to Brodsky's biographer, Lev Loseff, a cheer went up through the building.) So what was it that these lovely, brilliant people—and Medvedev is always aware, and I hope this comes through in the translations, that he is the bone of their bone and the flesh of their flesh—had missed? What was it that they hadn't known?

The answer was surprising. It turned out that the thing they hadn't known was the very thing they thought they knew best of all: Marxism. Not the Soviet "teachings of Karl Marx," but the many intellectual heirs of Marx in the West in the postwar era. This was the Frankfurt School and Sartre and the Situationist International and Pierre Bourdieu and the Anglo-American thinkers around the *New Left Review*; but also such non-aligned thinkers as Barthes, Foucault, and Baudrillard. It's not that these figures were entirely unknown in the Soviet Union, but that they were only partly known, or known in the wrong context. Sartre and Brecht, for example, were discredited among the anti-Soviet intelligentsia for their occasional kind thoughts about the Soviet Union and their willingness to turn a blind eye to Stalinism. It was, in a way, a bizarro world, where gentle, erudite, be-tweeded humanists could tell you that, well, under capitalism some people sink and others float, and the only other option was dictatorship and the Gulag. In the 1990s, in Russia, a lot of these people simply sank. Others adjusted.

It wasn't that the Russian intelligentsia didn't know that they were missing something. To the contrary: the crime of the Soviet regime was precisely that it had cut them off from what they called world culture. A key figure in this for Medvedev is Joseph Brodsky[1]. Brodsky, who himself managed to escape to the West, would write movingly of his generation's attachment to culture— what he called, quoting Osip Mandelstam, "a yearning for world culture." World culture, for Brodsky's generation, got through in dribs and drabs, and was hungrily consumed. "Nobody knew literature and history better than these people, nobody could write better Russian than they, nobody despised our times more profoundly," he famously wrote. And, having grown up around them, in Moscow and then in the United States, I would add: no one loved the Beatles more than these people; no one loved Fellini more; no one read Hemingway, Robert Frost, Jack London more carefully. So what had they missed? What had they failed to know?

---

1   See more on Brodsky in the Glossary of Names.

It was, in a way, their own history that they could not see, their own achievement. What Medvedev discovered was that the thing they'd missed was what had been under their noses all along.

This book presents a large portion of Medvedev's writings from the past decade. It includes his first published poems, from *It's No Good*; poems from his second book, *Incursion*; and then his essays, manifestos, and further poems, mostly from the period of his literary exile, gathered from published sources and also from his website (kirillmedvedev.narod.ru) and his LiveJournal account (zoltan-partosh.livejournal.com); more recently Medvedev has been posting new poems on his Facebook page, and those are also included here.

I don't know if our translations can capture the honesty, transparency, and passion of Medvedev's writing, both in his essays and in his poems, but we've tried. As all translators know, it is the plain style, the conversational style, that is often the hardest to capture. And Medvedev, though very much a student of Western writing and thought, is entirely focused on his Russian audience.

That audience now exists in a way that earlier it had not. When I first met Medvedev, in the spring of 2007, three and a half years after he left the literary world, a year after the publication without his permission of the NLO book, he started a DIY venture he called the Free Marxist Press[2]. Its entire staff consisted of Medvedev. Its first books were little stapled pamphlets by Western Marxists, often translated by Medvedev—Ernest Mandel, Herbert Marcuse, Pier Paolo Pasolini. They were printed by a copy shop on the fourth floor of an old apartment building in central Moscow. Medvedev met me one day at the Pushkin statue with a big ugly gym bag: he had just picked up the entire print run of one hundred copies of his own book, of essays and action reports, and he gave

---

2 Svobodnoe Marksistskoe Izdatel'stvo [*Свободное Марксистское Издательство*] is abbreviated by Medvedev, with an ironic subtext, as SMI [СМИ]—the acronym widely used by the "mass media" to refer to itself (i.e. "Sources of Mass Information").

me one. At the time he was regularly dismissed—as he writes here in his essay on Kuzmin—as a crazy person, a marginal person, a former writer.

In fact I think Medvedev is Russia's first genuinely post-Soviet writer. And I'm happy to report that he has returned, in his way, to the Russian literary world—but on his own terms. The Free Marxist Press has expanded—its first full-length book, Terry Eagleton's *Marxism and Literary Criticism*, translated by Medvedev, came out in 2010, and since then the press has published writings by Žižek, Badiou, the French sociologist and philosopher Michael Löwy, as well as Russian writers on revolutionary history, protest, and the Soviet dissident movement. It has grown in seriousness, prestige, and import, becoming, in effect, post-Soviet Russia's first independent left-wing publisher, putting out the works of its own people and those sympathetic to it, just as Medvedev calls for in "My Fascism." In late 2011 it published as a separate book a long, rhyming poem by Medvedev about interviewing Claude Lanzmann, the friend of Sartre and director of *Shoah*, on a visit he made to Moscow. In 2009 Medvedev founded a rock band, Arkady Kots—named after a Russian poet and socialist who translated the *Internationale* into Russian—which now plays with more regularity in Moscow and other cities, usually performing the poems of the art-terrorist Alexander Brener set to guitar and drums.

In the fall of 2011, Medvedev visited New York for the first time, and spent a few hours at the Occupy Wall Street encampment in Zuccotti Park. He was moved and excited by it, though he insisted that the movement needed demands. Two months later, I watched a YouTube video of Medvedev, at one of the big protests in Moscow, using the human mic to declaim a poem by a revolutionary Moldovan poet. A few months after that, he and a friend were singing Arkady Kots songs in a police van. In the spring of 2012, he was active in the Occupy Abai encampment in central Moscow, where, on May 12, Arkady Kots led the encampment in singing Medvedev's translation of the old Catalan antifascist song "L'Estaca."

I hope this book finds readers for whom Medvedev can begin to mean as much as he has meant to me these past six years.

—Keith Gessen, New York, October 2012

About the Second Edition:

Since the first edition of this book came out in 2012, Medvedev has not relented either in his critique or his activity, even as the pressure against activists has accelerated under an increasingly revanchist Putin regime. He has also remained adamant that he does not intend to leave Russia. For this second edition, we have made some minor corrections and added several poems responding to the crisis and war in Ukraine.

—K.G., November 2015

Note on the text:

Medvedev's punctuation in his poems, in particular with regard to capital letters, is highly idiosyncratic. Roughly speaking, the older he gets, the more capital letters he uses, and we have, almost entirely, followed the Russian original in this. In the essays, so as not to clog the text up with too many footnotes, we have made some adjustments for the sake of clarity. All the adjustments have, we hope, been done in the spirit of Medvedev, both politically and in terms of his demand that all editions of his work be pirate editions.

In sections where there are multiple translators, they have been indicated with initials after the individual poems.

All explanatory footnotes were added by the editor, unless noted otherwise.

IT'S NO GOOD [poems]

Selected poems from
It's No Good (Всё плохо)
Proekt OGI, 2000

Translations by Cory Merrill and Keith Gessen

\\\

I'm tired of translating
I probably won't translate
anymore
I think it's only worth doing
if you really feel
you can become one
with the author
sign on
to every line
pick up and amplify
his cry
that's how I felt
when translating
this one american,
charles bukowski,
a poet and novelist
I wanted as many people
as possible to hear him,
and understand just a little bit
of what, it seemed to me,
he understood
translating him
I felt there was no one
who understood him
as I understood him
even though we had nothing in common
neither on the inside
nor the outside
nor biographically
(and we still don't)
and charles bukowski isn't exactly my ideal
which is why I think
I spoke

in a voice that wasn't his voice
and this wasn't any kind of betrayal
(which it sometimes is with translators
who speak with someone else's voice
because they have no voice of their own)
I think it was genuine contact—
when two completely different people
begin to understand one another
in my opinion this
is a real event
in art and in life
I translated an entire novel
and many poems by bukowski
I did a good job
I don't know about the novel as a whole
but there are really brilliant passages—
I'm sure of that
the poems too
when I was translating the poems
of charles bukowski
I was convinced that I was writing
the best poetry then being written in russian
to be honest
I still think that
unfortunately I don't know
when it will be published
it's possible
it will never be published
and to be honest
I no longer care
because I know
someone else might translate
the novel and publish it earlier
with another publisher
and maybe it won't be a bad translation
but it won't reach the same heights

and in fact it could be a totally
disgraceful translation;
right now I'm translating a detective novel
for the prestigious journal *international literature*
it's for a new supplement
called, I think,
"books for the road"
I feel
like right now
I'm at the service
of the bourgeoisie
this detective novel was by john ridley
a black american writer
he's 32 years old
it's an action-packed novel
like a tarantino film
a satire of hollywood
and a critique of
the hollywood establishment
but with the use of
all the same tired hollywood cliches
in my opinion translators are
on the whole
with some rare exceptions
ghouls
feeding on
other people's blood
because translation is like
a sweet dream
whereas actually creating something
is torture
which is why
I will probably stop
working on
translations

tr. KG

\\\

just a little bit more about literature:
I've always been really interested
in a particular type of poet
it's a pretty well-known type:
fair-haired guys
who arrived in moscow
starting in the '30s
enrolled at the lit. institute[3]
raged through its dormitories
they were from the provinces
these were some very cool dudes
masters of nostalgia
and enigmatic fools;
I think the demand for them
was huge
because to the aging poets of the capital
they appeared as
a living conscience
their living conscience;
it seems to me
they really wanted
to occupy a kind of niche
like a singer from the country
languishing in the city;
I think
they also really wanted
to try on the mask of the god Lel[4];

---

3   The Gorky Literary Institute in Moscow. The only university in Russia devoted exclusively to the education of working writers (novelists, poets, and translators); it was founded in 1933 (three years before the Iowa Writers' Workshop) as part of Stalin's cultural program. Medvedev also studied there. "Lit. Institute" is the common colloquial abbreviation.

4   Lel is a Slavic god of love, equivalent to one of the Gemini twins in Greek mythology.

a dozen of them
lost their minds
many turned
into bums
and have since
gone begging
on strastnoy boulevard
(once or twice I saw
ragged muzhiks
there pacing the lengths of the benches,
reciting poems,
claiming they were former students
of the lit. institute)
a few of these boys
hanged themselves,
the rest sank into obscurity;
nikolai rubtsov[5]
was the most famous of them
although, of course,
with rubtsov it wasn't so simple
at some point he lived in petersburg
where he spent time with the petersburg aesthetes
and trained himself in various formalist
tricks
he admired brodsky
and so on
I think
everybody knows
that upon arriving in moscow
he was roped in
by these beekeepers
from the lit. institute,

---

5 Nikolai Rubtsov (1936–1971). Soviet lyric poet born in a village in the northern Arkhangelsk region, orphaned at a young age, served in the army, came to Leningrad after his demobilization, enrolled at the Gorky Literary Institute in 1962. Killed in a domestic dispute.

it seems to me
they stuffed him
into the framework of their odious myth
effectively destroying him
and then put out for all to see
a straw-stuffed scarecrow in the pantheon
even now
at the lit. institute
you can find
guys like this

tr. CM/KG

\\\

the summer before last
I got lost in berlin
this was in
tiergarten
I found myself
in an absolutely empty square
and all around was forest
and the square was empty
I saw a guy
riding his bike
and ran over to him
and asked in english
how to get to the center of town;
he was really happy to see me
because he turned out to be a russian immigrant
he got off his bike
and started giving me directions
to the center
in russian
in great detail;
the whole time he was describing
how to get to the center
his really unpleasant little kid
who was sitting on a metal rack
attached to the back of the bike
was behaving terribly
he moaned squealed growled
and cried,
he pulled my sleeve
and threw back his head
and rolled his eyes
(in russia, I thought to myself, they call kids like this
shilo v zhope, an awl in your ass);

the boy was obviously bored
because he couldn't understand
what we were saying,
and kept keening out something in german
(the same phrase over and over)
later on I figured out
what he kept saying
I think
he kept saying,
warum spricht Ihr nicht Deutsch?
that is,
"why don't you speak german?"
I was very moved
by this scene
with the russian immigrant.
I thought: "poor immigrant
he has no one to speak russian with—
and his son's a german!"
I think
this scene
struck me more than any other,
even more than the wild rabbits
I later saw in the center
of berlin
(even though I love
rabbits)
it struck me more
than the german girl, anna hennig,
who wrote about me in
the *berliner spiegel*
and even more than wonderful berlin itself,
that gigantic incessant construction site.

tr. KG

\\\

my friend misha
published an article in the magazine *afisha*[6]
but under someone else's name
that is they combined his text
with someone else's
(albeit with his permission)
when misha sent them an email
asking if he would receive
any payment,
the magazine sent back a one-word answer—
"no";
misha told me about this
and I was furious
I said to misha
that if *afisha*
did that to me
I'd burn all my bridges
and in fact I'd call them on the phone
and tell them very clearly what I thought of them
and their mothers,
so as to get at least
a little bit of fun
from the whole affair;
but misha is smart and patient;
he probably even figured out
some way
to turn this incident to his advantage;
misha is going to do everything right
in this life,
whereas I'm going to continue sitting here
deep in shit
with my principles.

tr. KG

---

6   *Afisha*: biweekly lifestyle and listings magazine founded in Moscow in 1999.

\\\

I've met a lot of people
who, hating themselves
for their cultured timidity,
try with all their might
to stamp it out of themselves;
this can manifest itself in different ways;
there is, for example,
the phenomenon of radicalism;
I've noticed
that many harmless young men
who look like sheep herders
(or, as one of my friends said
of these
pseudo-radicals:
"they should be out catching butterflies")
try to join the extreme left
or, at least,
make some unambiguous nods
in its direction;
another tendency
I've noticed
is the desire to squeeze every last drop
of any kind of cultural or intellectual value
out of themselves;
that is,
if a person is
from a family of writers or scholars,
from a family
of the ceremonious,
old-fashioned
intelligentsia
but takes up, for example, business, then
he without fail is going to

cheat, swindle, and curse
like no worker or sailor ever cursed
(and with much greater intensity than if he had, for example, been
    born to a family of businessmen,
been a hereditary businessman);
it seems to me there is in all this
a terrible anguish, a desire to overcome one's inheritance,
to tear it out of yourself;
or if a poet of middling talent happens, for example,
to edit the book pages for a newspaper,
then he will not
accept reviews
of books by poets he feels
are *much* more talented than he,
he will try with all his might to *suppress* them, he will
do it until his dying breath
if such a poet had lived
during soviet times, he would have been an
"engaged" soviet poet
who would have tried
with all his might to bring his competitors down,
would have schemed against them,
ratted them out,
turned them in to the KGB—of this I'm certain—
in general, it seems to me,
that in the brezhnev era, and also before it,
people could express their characters more clearly than now,
someone who at the time would have turned a fellow poet in
    (out of jealousy),
now simply would not accept a review of a book by that poet;
but someone else (especially if he is, for example, a famous
    prose writer
or news anchor
or even just a waiter)
is not going to respond to your request

to call him
(regarding your shared business)—
he is going to talk to you
as if you were an *asshole* and he a *divinity*
he is going to weasel out of his obligations
he thinks, apparently,
that he
can do anything
(and if he finally manages to rid himself of
all those cultured prejudices, all those *values*, then even more
    will be possible for him)
thus he will stall and equivocate the whole time
sometimes I start to think that
people conceal too much
that they are rude
and lie
too much;
sometimes I get the sense
that someone convinced them
(maybe as far back as childhood)
that there was no other way
that otherwise nothing
would come their way
and what's more
I don't really see anything in particular
happening for any of them
(we all
live
among losers)
people are generally too busy
satisfying their pathetic vanities
and petty ambitions
young men
need glory, power,
flowers, women, men;

girls need
prestige, comfort, satiety;
I have seen very few people
who *really* had something great going on
and I think that it has to do with the fact
that people lie and conceal
too much;
it's entirely possible
that if they were to stop
lying so much
and being rude
and equivocating about what they did
so often
then maybe something
would start to happen for them.

tr. CM

\\\

sickness:
all my life is
illuminated by sickness;
I see houses
and trees
in the dampish pale light of sickness;
when I walk through
the empty streets or courtyards
(or through other empty spaces)
I'm followed by its nauseating smell;
like many people
I have an idea for a novel
(an unrealized idea)
about a man whose whole life
(like my whole life)
is illuminated by sickness
(don't tell me, please don't tell me
that I'm being
dramatic; there's no need; I could say it
myself just as well, and it would be
partly true, but
I think that my consciousness
for reasons of its own
pumps these little doses of sickness
into my body
I think that it's something like the opposite
of anaesthesia,
a portion of pain that covers over or heals
emptiness);
yes,
everything tied to sickness is very important
to me
because I've understood a great deal

from it;
for example through death,
or, rather, through sickness I learned
how children understand death:
this was
five years ago
I was in the hospital
in the same ward as some soldiers
who were sick with yellow fever—
they had an epidemic of simple yellow fever
in their barracks—
whereas I had a much more sophisticated and dangerous,
chronic form of yellow fever
(a drug-addict's sickness!
kids, use clean, disposable needles)
and so I was lying with
these soldiers
in this white hospital ward
which resembled
a white barracks
and felt this diseased, inflamed organ
inside myself,
which I imagined was shiny
(I imagine the human liver
to be shiny—
like a cow's liver, for example,
which of course I've seen many times in stores
next to other cow parts—
this shiny mass, or breast,
entirely shiny, like a puddle)
anyway,
observing the soldiers,
listening to the stories
they told one another
and me,

I did the crossword with them,
I was able to guess the words
better than anyone else,
and so I very quickly achieved a kind of
intellectual stature
among them;
and it occurred to me there,
in the hospital,
that my liver is going to remain
this way
until I die;
the thing is,
you can imagine
that while you're alive
all sorts of things will change:
you'll grow new hair,
you'll shed your skin
and grow a new coat of skin
or
something will happen
with your nails
(or even your bones),
but something that's diseased
and can't be cured
will remain that way
till the end
(and it will be
like an aging wound);
that's when I thought about
why children don't fear death—
they think
they're going to die
as absolutely different people;
I think that they think
that by the time they're old enough

to die
everything about them will have changed,
and so it's as if this won't be
them dying
(I remember this about myself:
when I was little I thought
that when it came time for me to die
that everything would be different
and that it wouldn't be me anymore exactly
and so for me, in the form that I was then,
there was nothing to fear)
children think that
in the form
in which they now exist
they will live forever

tr. CM/KG

\\\

I really like when
a series of arches in moscow run
one after the other
creating their own kind of tunnel
out of arches
I know a place
on smolensky boulevard where
five arches run one after the other
creating a very long passage;
it's remarkable;
one day, admiring this tunnel,
this hollow
air channel
locked into the granite
I noticed one
of my old classmates
walking past me
with some boyfriend
she definitely recognized me, but didn't show it
(even though I hadn't changed at all—though she, she had
changed)
from then on, every time I pass by that composite tunnel
I remember
a few of the girls from school,
and, you know,
various
peers, both male and female,
but mostly
I remember the girls from school
beautiful girls
who enrolled in the Financial Academy
or got married to some wealthy caucasian[7];

---

7 Caucasian, in the Russian context, means someone from the Caucasus
region (Chechnya, Georgia, Azerbaijan, Armenia, etc.).

there was
a time when
they were certain, for some reason,
that before anything else they had to figure out
how to provide for themselves
that is
how to make money
or, if they were lucky, get married;
only then
could you concern yourself with what you were
genuinely interested in
grad school, for example, or art, or family,
I don't know
who taught them that;
it's possible
that this wasn't just a fad in school then,
but that these murderous ideas
were spewing forth
from the very air;
some of these girls really did get married
to rich, hideous caucasians,
or to rich, hideous
russians;
some, I think,
had children with the husbands of other women
(also rich and talented)
the most beautiful and talented girls
corrupted to the core long ago
by their uselessness
their emptiness
and so what I'm talking about has nothing to do with
children
or
family harmony, or
petty tranquility, vegetative satisfaction

(with satiety—yes, but a kind of meaningless satiety,
and so more like gluttony)
by the way, some, I think, are still having kids
out of a sense of doom,
in order to
break away
from their inner emptiness
although I doubt
they will succeed
in breaking away from that suffocating emptiness,
nothingness
smoke and chaos
only
heavy, swirling smoke, chaos,
only a useless swirling
between night clubs,
shoe stores,
and home;
some of the girls from my class had already been with
a lot of men even then
I try to imagine how many men
they had had;
for inspiration
I buy
a small cheese-filled
pie
I walk past the borovitzkaya metro stop
where I sold books five years ago;
I walk further,
past the place
in front of the lenin
library
where I sold ice cream
five years ago
I walk further,

thinking about how
my poems
are the poems of an *unemployed* person
(as opposed to, say, the poems of the poet
stanlislav lvovsky[8],
which he sent me not long ago:
his, in my opinion, are
the opposite—
a person in his poems is always
returning from work
moving around the glaring twilit
cityscape
given shape by information streams—I don't know
how you can sense it—but
reading those poems, you're left
with that kind of feeling).
I think about how
self-sufficiency
and dignified aloofness are qualities foreign to me
I think
I need involvement;
I thirst for some kind of confluence;
having forgotten that tunnel
(which stirred in me, by the way,
in addition to everything else,
a kind of fixed, if not ruinous,
obsession,
evoking the image
of some delightful, ruinous chill
of breathing a cool freedom
of some kind of heavy, low flight
a feeling that

---

8   Stanislav Lvovsky (1972–). Contemporary of Medvedev's; associated with
Vavilon poets. See more about Lvovsky in Medvedev's essay "Dmitry Kuzmin" on
pages 184–186.

43

comes over me pretty often of late
it's a kind of knowledge
that lies like a lump
in my soul;
I sometimes wonder
where it comes from
and cannot understand;
in the end I think
it's the kind of knowledge
that comes from without, like a blow)
I am surprised
that it worked out like this
I'm even a little terrified by it
I cannot understand
why I should feel
so lucky
the luckiest
of everyone,
of everyone
who ended up marrying a rich caucasian
or left for the united states
and is working there
for the *washington post*
sometimes coming in on business trips
and staying at the National
of everyone who turned out to be a computer genius
of everyone who became an assistant
to editors-in-chief
or a designer
for major fashion magazines
and of everyone who became
editors-in-chief
of such magazines
of everyone who finished their studies at the Medical Institute
of everyone who, the day before his wedding,

fucked some black girl for two hundred dollars
with his friends, the five of them, in a car
in the alley next to tverskaya
(for those who don't know, this is called a "bachelor party")
of all the historians
the students of god,
those who didn't get into the Financial Academy
and worked their way up, and became managers
of wine depots
of everyone who got married,
traded in their parents' apartment,
and were separated by the fourth day
of all the half-drunk and stunted intellectuals
who (unlike me)
matured too early,
then burned out
of everyone who found work in the morgue
of everyone who did time in jail
then died of an overdose
of everyone who worked at
the politician kirienko's campaign headquarters
and then joined his permanent team.

tr. CM

\\\

I don't know why
I decided to work
at the nightclub Sexton
when I was eighteen
they didn't pay very much
(true, it was better than collecting
empty bottles off the street); I worked there
as a janitor.
at the time, there weren't very many
nightclubs in moscow
but this was definitely
a place apart
in those days the club was ruled
by the Night Wolves;
for those who don't know,
this was a kind of
savage semi-criminal
organization,
a hired motorcycle gang;
it was actually pretty dangerous
to work in that club
it was a very
shady
place;
there was this one incident
with my friend Yan
who also worked there as a janitor:
one day, having worked the night shift,
he lay down just before dawn to rest
(you could sleep there late at night
after the customers had basically all left
or fallen asleep on the benches—
we also could sleep on the benches)

and so, having worked the whole night,
Yan lay down on a bench
but at some point got up
to use the bathroom
from where he heard shots
and returning
noticed
that his leather jacket
which he had just been wrapped up in while sleeping
was riddled
with bullet-holes;
among the Night Wolves
was a guy
they called Che;
he wasn't their formal leader
(they had a leader who went by the name of Surgeon—
a former dentist)
but he still commanded
a great deal of respect
among them;
I didn't quite understand
where this respect came from;
the truth is, he was the
shyest among them
and what's more he stuttered
(by the way, it's possible
that it was precisely for these two reasons
that he posessed such authority
I very strongly felt the respect
the unspoken although very great
piety
they all felt toward him
and it was clear
that behind it all was
a kind of power, an incomparable

force)
one day one of the customers at the club
approached me and asked
where he could get a
prostitute around here
I said that I didn't know
he looked at me carefully
and asked:
*"What are you doing here,
jewish child?"*
I said that I worked
here
(I decided then
that he must have been some very high-ranking
jewish gangster
because it was clearly with sympathy
that he had asked);
from time to time
in that club
there were raids by the police
people in masks
would burst in,
make everyone
get down on the floor,
and be searched
when these raids were going on
some of the girls at the club
would pass me drugs
or syringes;
I'd hide them in the bathroom
or flush them down the toilet—whatever the person wanted
(I was never searched;
as a janitor
I was always beyond suspicion)
once a girl

whom I'd just cleaned a table for
(she was wearing a short leather jacket and
leather pants)
told me that she had worked all day
and had come here to relax
(I didn't believe
that she had worked all day;
she clearly belonged to the Night Wolves
and they were obviously able to make sure
their women
didn't have to work
I think she just told me that
because she felt awkward in front of me, going back and forth
   between chairs
at that particular moment)
she told me she loved akhmatova
and bella akhmadulina
(or tsvetaeva and akhmadulina
I'm not exactly sure
but she definitely mentioned
akhmadulina[9])
I didn't really understand
why she decided to tell me
this;
but I liked that girl at that moment
(I know this because
I still remember
what I was wearing
that night;
when you realize you like someone
you notice what you're wearing
and you remember it

----

9   Anna Akhmatova and Marina Tsvetaeva—major poets of the Russian Silver
Age. Bella Akhmadulina, popular poet from the 1960s.

because at that moment you are looking at yourself
as though with her eyes
the eyes of the person you like,
I've noticed).
The Night Wolves
wore black leather jackets
and leather pants
got to the club
at night
settled their
affairs
and drank
until morning
(just like pirates, I thought);
the Sexton for me
was like a highly concentrated version of life
these days I live
an unnatural life,
yesterday I went to the metro
took the escalator down
and almost fainted;
it was like I was hysterical
I really terrified people;
to me, it felt like
that entire mass of people
was literally pressing on me
with their neuroses;
it was as though I had turned up
inside a crowd of human neuroses;
it was
a miasma of anxieties
(arguments with wives, with lovers, low wages,
the sickness or death of a parent, an addict son);
to me it all
seemed strange,

the thing is, I generally enjoy
large gatherings of people
I actually feel pretty good
in the middle of crowds; I could remember
something like this happening to me only once before
a few years ago;
I stepped into a big book store
and it felt like
that entire mass of people
was all pressing on me
with their neuroses;
it seems
this sort of thing
is going to be happening to me pretty often now;
I think this is largely because
I live a pretty unnatural life
I go through life now
as a professional writer
I haven't had the kind of job
I had back then at the Sexton
for a very long time
but after that incident in the metro
I thought maybe I'd look for
some kind of job like that again

tr. CM

\\\

not so long ago, my girlfriend Anisa and I
were at a party
with, for the most part,
the young bourgeois intelligentsia—
designers, journalists from popular magazines,
and so on,
and Anisa admitted to me afterward
that she's bored by such company,
and I said to her, "Not to worry,
before long you're going to see something
straight out of dostoevsky,
with no chaser";
and sure enough
a few days later we showed up at a birthday party
for one of my old friends,
with a group of talented failures,
where the hostess, the birthday girl,
went into hysterics
screaming in front of everyone
that she was going to divorce her husband;
she lunged at him,
alleging that he had tried to beat her up
the night before;
she cursed him
for drinking too much,
drinking away her wages,
and for reading only newspapers
I listened to all this
and was shaken
I was trembling
from weakness and
helplessness,
from the impossibility

of anyone being comforted,
of anyone being helped—
not her, not myself, and not him,
her husband,
especially not him.

tr. CM

INCURSION

[poems]

Selected poems from
Incursion (Вторжение)
Argo-Risk, 2002

Translations by Bela Shayevich and Keith Gessen

\\\

holy lonely creatures
lost and late
castaway hungry lowly
miserable
lonely unfeeling dirty
dishonest useless
discarded
smeared on the wall
eaten with shit
I remember an incident:
last summer
I was standing next to the pushkin movie theater
and not far from me
were a couple of men
with very relaxed
lackeyish mannerisms
I thought they might be taxi drivers
waiting for pick-ups
after the last show
I was also waiting for somebody
I decided to ask them
the time
one of them said
"it's over there"
and nodded in the direction of a street clock
not far from where we were standing
I said
"what does it say—I can't see it"
and he told me
"I can't see it either"
"do you see it?"
I asked the other one
and he told me

"no I don't see it either"
why am I telling
this story
I know exactly why
I am telling this story
because
I was really into
that situation
it literally made me
ecstatic
I almost thought to myself
long live myopia!
everyone wants to feel like
they are strong and important
and if not, if this is, for example,
too much responsibility for someone
then they want the opposite to be true
they want to feel like they are
dejected
a castaway
useless
they want to turn to somebody and say
"LISTEN TO ME!"
thirsting for beer and for vodka
thirsting for
normal human interaction
LISTEN TO ME!
miserable castaway damned;
proud
myopic
hungry lowly
numbed;
lonely holy
precious mumbling and dumbfounded
boiled alive

smeared on the wall
wiped off the face of the earth.

tr. BS

\\\

these are just little poems and nothing else
(—stanislav lvovsky) this is just
another poem
that will most likely
not say anything new
and definitely not say
anything much
this poem will most likely
be indistinguishable from
all the other poems
I've written this year
it will be more
of the same:
I have the feeling that
lately somebody
has been
short-changing me;
I have the feeling that lately
somebody has not been letting me get in somewhere;
often, I'm moved by the feeling
that I broke something that belongs to somebody
and that is why now somebody is
not letting me
do something;
a little more
a little more of the same;
after a reading at a club in moscow
a poet told me:
"Kirill, you should change your *method*
it's getting stale,"
and I told him yes, yes, I'd noticed that, too
I see what you're saying and, you know, I am already searching for
    (*already* searching for!)

some new *approaches*, subjects, *intonations*,
so it'll soon be different, soon
everything will be good again, just be patient a little more, please
a little more
a little more
(of the
same)
among the various conjectures, rumors about me
going around the OGI club that evening
there were many conflicting opinions:
someone, for example, was convinced
that I'd burnt out,
others believed
that I had become
hopelessly, feverishly prolific, a third
that my poems were "shit"
that what I wrote weren't poems, THEY WERE NOT
poetry;
I have noticed that many women
are often unsatisfied with things about
their husbands and lovers; for example,
my girlfriend Anisa recently asked me,
"why don't you read any good literature,
why is everything you read such crap?"
I told her, "reading too much is bad for you."
but I should have said
"I don't like
good literature"
the fact of the matter is that lately I really
have not been into good literature
I have noticed that
many women
are completely unsatisfied with the intelligence
of their husbands and lovers,
one woman

spent a long time talking to me (or rather, not to me
but *near me*) about
some guy that she found
really pathetic because he only thought about what was trendy, about
consumption
("*it's not even consumption,*" she told me,
"*because in the desire to consume, at least there is some passion*
(fear, anxiety, excitement—K.M.) *but he*
lacks even that")
I was listening to all this
and thinking
that she was probably talking about
some acquaintance of hers
that she had interacted with for a sum total
of a day or so, but it turned out she was talking about her husband
with whom she had lived for seven or eight
years;
this was amazing to me;
at one point, my loser-photographer friend Zhenya started handing
    out business cards
that said "Zhenya Yakimenko, photographer," with his phone
    number,
to any girl he saw that he liked (on the street, at a club, in the metro)
and most of the girls that he gave his card to
ended up
calling him,
even the ones who seemed completely jaded,
by no means lacking male attention, even ones who had steady
    lovers or husbands (or both) and seemed generally satisfied with
    their lives
why?
why did they all end up calling him?
I said, "Zhenya, by my count something like 20 out of 30 girls
    called you," and he said,
"yes, and 18 of them want me

to help solve
some problem of theirs";
and I said, "Zhenya, maybe
they just want you to entertain them?"
(the bored women
who need some sort
of entertainment)
some of them
entertain
themselves
one of the girls who called Zhenya was named Gabby,
she was bisexual;
Zhenya said that for a long time he couldn't understand
why she spoke such good
Russian (considering the fact that she didn't read newspapers
or books)
"then I figured it out," he told me, "Gabby spends a lot of time
interacting with homosexuals
and homosexuals usually speak really good, pure
Russian";
another of the girls
who called Zhenya, he
told me, he couldn't understand
how such a dim intellect could be
placed in such
a beautiful body
(which really is strange);
for some reason when one
person tells stories, they can seem
completely uninteresting
but when another person—Zhenya, for instance—tells these
  anecdotes, talks about these kinds of incidents
they become
very interesting, and, most importantly,
any detail from them

becomes practically a confession and
emanates a sort of viscous, unctuous, nervous, delirious
light
I thought to myself that probably
this was because certain people know how
to choose correctly
yes, this is probably because they know how to choose correctly
we dance around others' misfortunes like mischievous wolves like
    some sort of
lascivious bats in a frenzy
we make our way toward them by the light of bonfires on the
    outskirts of town
through desolate fields of garbage
we fall on them swoop down throw ourselves at them with all of
    our might oozing
the syrupy poison of empathy

tr. BS

\\\

in the Smolensky supermarket
at the corner of the Garden Ring
and Arbat
among the piles
of expensive
luxurious
foods
I found a sprat paté
for seven rubles;
on the can it said
it contained pearl-barley
I took two
figuring
this must be a special delivery
for neighborhood residents
who come to the store
every day
and aren't anywhere as rich
as the fat middle-aged men
who come here in their cars
from other neighborhoods
to load up on groceries
for real
I took the paté
and started walking alongside
the shelves of products;
I wanted to find some inexpensive
fish
and I looked and looked
at these beautiful foods
lying there on these
shelves
and at the magazines

which looked very odd
against the background of all this food
I walked around
for so long
that the guards
keeping an eye out for thieves
grew tired of watching me
it was very beautiful there
and I liked it;
I remember
I didn't pay much attention
to the other customers
they didn't really interest me
especially as
there weren't so many of them
they walked around
hardly looking
placing
the products into these rolling baskets
whereas I
very carefully
piously
studied every single item
and read their
exotic names
these magnificently packaged meals
they could make your head spin
(there was for example
a product called
"two rainbow trouts")
I wandered around so long
that toward the end
I developed a strange
feeling;
it was something like

longing;
it was
a terrible
suffocating longing
and pity;
I was very sorry
for these fish
this wine
several hundred types of wine
and all the cookies
and the magazines
the candies
giant boxes of candies
massive pieces of meat
and fish;
and I looked for a long time
at these
idiotic beautiful expensive
toys
lying there
on the shelves
of that supermarket
and I thought that this probably was
the main fuel
of civilization
(not because we all live in a
consumer culture,
but simply because
everything else
is just noise
whereas food
say what you will about it
is protein
food is the main guarantee
of family happiness and prosperity

everything happens
because of food
and so there's probably
nothing surprising about the fact
that families collapse because of it
lovers part over it
and murders are committed
because of it);
walking around a bit more
I thought of the fact
that the suffocating pity I feel
for these products
is also
a form of fetishism
and also a symptom
of reification;
therefore it probably doesn't make sense
to feel sorry
for these products
that cause all these things
to happen;
I bought some fish fillets
and two cans
of that incredibly cheap paté
which I named
"paté for the poor";
walking out of the supermarket
with these products
I thought of how often
in my confrontations
with the face
of the society of consumption
sentimentality replaces disgust.

tr. KG

\\\

all the film critics in moscow
who attend press
screenings
are familiar with the group of people
they refer to as
"schizocinephiles";
these are strange-looking unkempt
men
half-insane
fifty or sixty years old
who go to every new movie;
they somehow find out about
these free press screenings
sometimes they get press passes
from some marginal
publications;
and they're snobs;
once,
I was standing outside the Museum of Film
and they were standing nearby, discussing the
program of the Moscow
Film Festival
and at some point one
of them tried
to involve me
in their conversation
but I, thankfully,
stepped off to the side;
that was when I saw them
for the first time:
all of them
have nicknames that the film critics
gave them behind their backs

one of them is Hippo;
recently, on the way to the Illusion movie theater,
a film critic told me, "Hippo
lost it the other day";
they say Hippo
moonlights as a nude model at the Surikov Art Institute;
the day in question he was very worked up
at the theater
he jumped from his seat, ran
to the cashier, screaming
"Shame on you! Where are the heads?
What's wrong with you!
This is a disgrace!"
(it was later explained to me
that he was referring to the projection being a bit crooked
which caused the top part of the shots to get cut off)
then at some point in the middle of the movie
(as a film critic who had been sitting next to him
told me later)
he fell asleep and began to snore very loudly
(I understand why this happened
it happens to me
too, from time to time,
the more engaging a movie is, the
more I want to sleep—the reaction
of a weak, over-refined psyche
to the triumph of art),
and so he fell asleep and started snoring loudly.
there's also one they call Masturbator;
there's a man
they call Toad,
though I don't know
anything about him;
there's Hitler, of course,
who teaches at the Moscow State Institute of Culture

(the most interesting thing about these guys is
that they come from various levels of society
from the real, as they say, dregs to the more or less socially
    adapted—the professors, for example—but all of them look
    exactly the same and, most importantly, smell the same)

— — —

Masturbator always carried
a beautiful but worn alligator-skin briefcase
he would pull pens out of to write things down
during movies;
once
a cashier
said something disparaging to him
about his briefcase;
he tried to protest,
but she
shut him down,
and after that
he started
going downhill—
he lost weight,
stopped coming to the movies and press screenings as often
and even appeared
without his beautiful briefcase
sometimes;
a critic recently told me
that Masturbator had died.
this is all very interesting
I have a lot to say about all this
I really empathize
with these cinephiles
I think these are the ancient specters of art,
these are the doomed spirits walking among us,

for me, they represent everything
fevered
about art and its surroundings:
the fanaticism,
the snobbery,
the silly
obsession, the baseless
sense of some sort of philanthropy,
community
or
superiority;
I believe
that these are
the fevered specters of art
that speak in declarations
art isn't this, isn't that
art isn't this or that or that
art is a fistfight in the orchestra pit
art is God knows what at this point
art is not, in any case, Verlaine and Rimbaud
in a bar in Belgium
most likely, art is a wife who does not share or partake in
your interests, it's your young son
an insensitive idiot, cretin
(I remember
how
when one of my friends was a teen
he wrote
"DAD IS A BASTARD"
on the wall of his room)
this, this is basically how I imagine it:
art is noise, howling, barking
weeping swearing in the foyer;
it's perfectly possible that art is God knows what
I think that art is a fight in the orchestra pit

those schizocinephiles sometimes remind me
of the insane stamp collectors
I used to buy stamps from when I was a kid
they are also something like
elderly soccer fanatics
overall, I consider them a wonderful, nostalgic, dying type,
tragic,
the carriers of a disappearing character
the schizocinephiles—
who sense before everyone else
the falling of souls
and a drop in the temperature.

tr. BS

\\\

I recently ran into the poet Lvovsky
whose poems I like
(and he likes mine back)
on an escalator;
Lvovsky was going down and I was going up
I was chewing gum
and at the moment
we saw each other
I was blowing
a giant bubble;
our eyes met
and we smiled at one another;
I was curious what he thought
looking at me;
I was later told that on that very day
maybe
a day before or a day after that
people were discussing my poetry
on some website
and Lvovsky went on there with them
people were saying things like
when medvedev was young
his father sold off his huge collection of books
and the boy was left
without a good eduction
without an awareness of the
history of russian free verse;
I was told
that Lvovsky
· in a very subtle and restrained manner
talked to these people
and told them where to get off;
this stuff really gets to me;

I'm not a star
I'm not some diva poet
I'm not a disturber of the peace
I'm not *a professional*
I can't understand
why everything has been charged in this way—
"I stand among jokes and caresses"
as one of my favorite poets, Leonid Gubanov[10], once wrote;
the story of how and why my dad sold his books
should be its own poem sometime;
another story that needs to be told
is about how a pet rat bit my penis;
when people ask me
whether everything I write is true
I usually say
"yes, of course it's all true
do you really think
that I would make
this shit up?"—
the most important thing is
the most important thing is for a person to know their worth;
a person who knows his worth
a man who knows his worth
a woman
who knows her worth
that's what interests me the most
at this moment
in this place we have ended up in
it's essential to know
your own worth;
in the world that we live in

---

10   Leonid Gubanov (1946–1983). A non-conformist poet and founder of
SMOG, a neo-avant-garde literary circle. Gubanov was forcibly hospitalized at
a mental institution because of the group's public readings, political activity, and
connections to the dissident movement.

it is very important
(it is completely imperative)
to be complete and whole
like a poplar tree, birch, oak, like fuzz or an axe
or like an animal—
cat or a rooster
or like an elephant
or a dog
dying in the metro
when we're coming back
from somebody's house
tired, beautiful, tipsy
dressed absurdly
aging
immortal
I can't understand
why the fuck everyone is so upset
anonymous internet trolls
critics
journalists
lousy little poets
("*lousy little poets*," in the words of Leonard Cohen
little poets crawling with lice)
dull
(*gray*; or as they would say about themselves
gray as the lining of a coat—I don't like metaphors) critics
who write
that what's lacking in my poems
according to them
is some kind of depth of experience
jesus christ
depth of experience
(I think that wanting depth of experience from a poem
means not having any inkling of your own worth)
I want everyone to calm down, come to their senses

and the issue here isn't that I, for example, imagine I am
IMAGINE I AM
MAYAKOVSKY
BIG POWERFUL BEAST
NAGGED AT BY MY PATHETIC
CONTEMPORARIES
it feels like I've
somehow or other told everyone or a lot of people that
they are shit
(or something along those lines)
and I said it
in some strange manner
inadvertently
and I said it
because it turns out that I am also pathetic, powerless, weak
I think
that my poems are some kind of test;
a trial
for perfection or rather a test
to determine the capacity for perfection
to determine
THE CAPACITY
to see and accept yourself
as you are;
miserable, ugly, worthless,
vain, selfish,
head hanging low over a vast space
over some sparkling stinking abyss
(I think that for somebody hanging over a stinking abyss—
and the majority of people are—
"deep thoughts" are
beside the point)
excuse me for talking about myself so much
I think that soon I will probably stop talking about myself so much
I even have some idea, more or less, of how to kick

this habit
and sorry too for swearing
I really try not to swear in my poems
because I think that everything you want to express
can be done without swearing
this text should be dedicated to the problem of communication
and the core of this composition should have been the bubble
the bubble-gum bubble
but everything shifted somehow
and got mixed up
here's what I wanted to say:
sometimes the lack of human interaction can make a person
    physically ill
but sometimes human interaction is even worse than that
and since not all is lost yet
since some people still believe in us
and because some still consider us
the voice of our generation
(and because we are, in the end, still standing)
I would like once more to emphasize that:
we are lonely
very few people believe in us
we are reluctant to show our poems
to our parents, to our close friends, our acquaintances
no one believes in us
after a good day at work
no one will go have a beer with us
no one will teach us loneliness

tr. BS

\\\

last summer my girlfriend Anisa and I
went to petersburg
we stayed in a room
that her friend Anya was renting
in some industrial neighborhood,
off the Narvskaya metro stop;
it's a neighborhood of
small two-
and three-story buildings,
with
a couple of apartments
in each;
there are many
empty sandlots;
the buildings in that neighborhood
are literally drowning in foliage,
people hang their laundry
under their windows;
the man who owned the apartment
where Anya was renting a room
was older
around sixty
a retired geologist;
the apartment
was in pretty
bad shape;
Anya was letting
us stay in her room
because she
was in
moscow;
we had gotten to petersburg in the morning
in the evening we went to the apartment

to sleep
and at night,
after we had gone to bed,
the old man
brought two whores
back to the aparment;
they were both around fifty;
these were hardened old whores,
and the three of them
spent a long time sitting
in the kitchen
talking
and I think
drinking vodka
and then
the three of them
went out into the corridor
right in front of our door
and the whores started
trying to talk the old man into
some kind of
transaction
(I think
they were trying to convince him
to trade his apartment
for another apartment
or to register both of them
at his apartment
or something along those lines);
the old man refused
they insisted
"who's in this room?"
they asked
and he said
"boarders"

I was glad
Anisa was asleep
because at a certain point
I became convinced
that any minute now
they would start threatening the old man
and then kill him
and then come in and kill
the "boarders";
finally the old man told the whores
that he'd do what they want
and sign off on
the deal
but only if they slept with him
right then and there
(both of them);
he spent a long time
talking them into it
he promised them
ten orgasms apiece
(those were his exact words)
but the whores
refused;
they told the old man:
"first let's make it official
then we'll fuck you"
in the end
they didn't
agree on anything;
the whores
left toward morning;
the next night
Anisa and I
decided not to
stay there again

and spent the night
at this guy Kostya's
apartment,
I don't remember
what metro stop it was;
things like this
happen in petersburg
all the time;
however after *this one incident* with the landlord
and the whores
I understood for the first time
that Dostoevsky didn't need to
make up his plots and his characters—
his beautiful elaborate plots
(the mere recollection of which
fills me
not only with an ice-cold terror but also with awe)
were spawned by this "intentional," as he said,
city;
I think there is something mystical about the fact
that all of this happened to us
the very first night we were there
although I am far from a mystic
so far from one
as far as a doctor would be, for example,
on the other hand I think that doctors in particular are no
    strangers
to mysticism, doctors today
still have something of the shaman about them
which is exactly why I couldn't be
a doctor
but if I suddenly turned into one I wonder what kind of body
    I would be entrusted with
most likely one that's half-dead, poisoned with drugs and
    anesthesia

and in any case, it wouldn't belong to the woman
Lawrence Durrell described in a letter to Henry Miller
"whose sex responses start upwards from the soles of her feet,"
and it wouldn't be the Russian language, which I do whatever
    I want with
and which in turn does whatever it wants with me.

tr. BS

EUROPE [poem]

Composed in October 2002, on the road to and from a poetry
festival in Rome, this would be Medvedev's last published poem
before he left the literary world. He refers to its composition in
"My Fascism." The original is untitled.

Published at Vavilon.ru
March 2003

Translation by Keith Gessen

I'm riding the bus
with a group of athletes
from some provincial town
they're going to a competition in Milan;
our bus has stopped at the border,
and waits to go through customs.
what country are we entering? one of them asks me;
Poland, I say.
so that's what, the EU? he asks.
no, I say. Poland's not in the EU yet.
what other countries are we going through?
Germany, I say, Austria
he nods
Portugal, I lie; he nods again;
I could have said Greece, Syria, Ireland—he'd have
nodded.
oh, mighty athlete,
our bus will travel through Iceland,
we'll see sheep, deer,
muskoxen;
we'll see camels;
we'll see the early ice—
hills of not quite solid,
not yet formed
(they call it
"uncrystallized")
but very real, early ice;
we'll see the Alps—they'll be
to both sides of us—
there'll be some nice places to cool off;
we'll see the ruins of Thebes, and the remains
of mad Alexandria—
but we won't look at any of this;
instead we'll watch movies
on our disc players;

we've been watching movies the whole way from Moscow,
one was an American film in which it gradually became clear
that using the shampoo Head and Shoulders was the only way
to save yourself from the alien invaders
(at the end, it turns out the film has actually been
an epic shampoo commercial)[11],
and just now we watched an old Soviet film
about World War II,
the action takes place around here somewhere—
I am ground, over, over, come in, this is ground, over, the
    communications officer says,
she is a pretty young officer,
but no one answers, they're dead (they're gone),
they've been killed,
though not before communicating the movement of the Nazi
    troops,
and their impending attack
from the northwest,
I cried over this "I am ground, over, over, come in, this is ground,"
I'd had a lot to drink on the road from Moscow to Minsk,
but I would have cried even if I hadn't had a single drop
between Moscow and Minsk;
I remembered the poet Lvovsky, who said he cried when he
    watched *Amelie*,
why did people love this Amelie
so much?
is it that they're so hungry
for some ordinary magic?
it's silly to explain that people liked it
just because they were hungry for magic
but there's no time, and no chance,
to explain why they really liked it;

---

11   *Evolution* (2001), sci-fi comedy starring David Duchovny and Julianne Moore.

there's a very popular, very stupid new word—*positivity*
(it's an idiotic word—and very popular);
politicians like to use it, and television personalities,
you'll hear dishwashers in restaurants using it, and policemen,
though often you'll hear them using its opposite,
they'll say, "*Negativity*—there's a lot of negativity around,"
meaning that there's not quite enough positivity,
and positivity is really what they need.
I also need positivity, because positivity, it seems to me,
is something like goodness,
but if I were to cry at *Amelie*, I'd cry because
goodness,
if it exists,
exists only in some forms
that are impossible for me to reach,
that are suspicious, skittish, awkward,
unreachable,
goodness exists if it exists
in some mangled new form,
in awful places,
in cold hellish places,
in wandering, dreaming, unstable
places
it exists, if it exists,
in diseased idiots,
plagued outcasts,
foolish ideas,
other people's annoying children,
blind invisible people—
in the form of tiny children
with big ears,
lumps,
unreachable, impossible, but absolutely specific,
visible but ultra-refined
forms

(and maybe this is exactly what Lvovsky was crying about—
if this is what I was crying about,
I wouldn't be crying about it
for the first time)
and so these forms
that have nothing to do with everyday life,
that have nothing to do with decorative forms,
that have nothing to do with one another,
or with the non-existent retro-music
that plays in the background while Amelie
performs her good deeds in Paris
(which also, incidentally, doesn't exist—
even if people have seen it,
and not just individual people but couples,
and not just once but two or three or four
times)—
a drunken Nazi is captured by the army, and he keeps saying
    something, begging
them not to kill him, because, he says, he's not a Nazi, at least
not a member of the SS, he's a communist, a worker from Leipzig,
he says;
the snow has stopped falling;
a Nazi is a Nazi
if one of my men was wounded during a reconnaissance misssion
I don't think I'd carry him back,
though I don't know;
how much longer are we going to stand here?
I'm in Belarus;
from the ride through Belarus I am left with the following
    impressions:
snow was falling, it had started falling pretty suddenly,
and you got the sense that nature was surprised,
the fields and the forests hadn't had time to stand there,
    beautifully, all through autumn,
and grow red and brown and lose their foliage,

and were surprised,
you could sense this surprise
in them;
October 7, 1941
(exactly sixty-one years ago),
there was a sudden snowfall here
the Germans hadn't thought the snow would come so early,
they were caught off guard, and this in the end spelled their doom
I imagine them wandering aound here, proud, brave, but a little
      bewildered,
looking at the snow and saying
"Scheisse"
(and I want to say to them, this isn't *scheisse*, this isn't shit,
it's *sneg*, snow,
s-n-o-w,
white, beautiful),
though sometimes scheisse is more beautiful
than "snow"
(and this seems indeed
to have been one such time),
but that wasn't here
and it wasn't
now,
here and now it was different,
this wasn't in Belarus,
this was something I learned in school,
though it wasn't something I was supposed to have learned, I
      think,
right here and now a part of the young Belarussian intelligentsia
with the help of their bald fuhrer Lukashenko
is bringing Belarus back to approximately the 6th century
and inventing a language
that from here on out the entire nation
is supposed to speak,
the principal goal being to invent words that don't exist

in Russian, or Polish, or Ukrainian
(instead of pants, *nagavitsi*, "leg-ons"),
and in theory I'd love to be part of such a process,
to create a language from scratch that, a few years hence,
my entire small nation will speak,
I think I'd really enjoy that[12];
immigration—everyone's worried about immigration
the Arabs and the Turks (Arabs in Paris and Marseilles, Russians
   and Turks in Germany)
versus that old fart Le Pen,
a lot of people these days
find themselves voting for fascists or
quasi-fascists;
it's said that in Germany this year
a quasi-fascist almost won the election;
for every white German that's born
three or four Arabs or Turks are born,
and it seems that the gentle German burghers
find this very disturbing;
the wonderful middle class consumers of various countries and
   nations

---

12   In the original publication at Vavilon.ru, this passage had the following
footnote appended to it: "From the editors: Most readers probably don't know the
contemporary Belarussian situation very well, and we therefore believe it impor-
tant to point out that the depiction of the situation in the poem does not accord
with reality. Views on the linguistic and cultural side of the matter differ, and the
ones expressed by Kirill Medvedev in this text are quite common, though a good
argument could be made for the other side. However the political aspect of the
case as presented by Medvedev is simply incorrect: those forces and tendencies in
Belarussian society that have been trying to create a new national language are
not only not supported by Lukashenko, they are his active opponents. Since we
believed this fact changed matters significantly, we asked the author to correct
the text; Kirill Medvedev, however, answered that this deviation from the truth
solved certain artistic questions that he was addressing in this composition. We
will probably be devoting a future article to this question, as well further delin-
eating the author's viewpoint and that of the editorial staff." http://www.vavilon.
ru/diary/030301.html

some part of the active Catholics and Orthodox
and writers and poets, not unlike me,
find this disturbing;
because they want to be read in a hundred years,
and they think that someone might stamp on (or devour)
their wonderful, shining,
their creepy
rotten
their maddening, genius (!)
language,
their rotten
gentle
dying culture,
the cocksucker mafia that runs America
is gradually conquering the entire world,
the Arabs and Turks
the Chinese, the blacks,
the Arabs,
Turks, Chinese,
the Chinese who are taking the world block by block
(the process begins with just a few Chinese on your block,
and then in a few years all the signs on your block are in Chinese,
and then it's a Chinese block)
the great migration of peoples
is simultaneously
the great mating
of peoples,
and a great pulling-down
that's what it is
a gigantic rupture
a secret crash
a terrible temptation
tempting us somewhere
but we won't give in,
although we're not just not

giving in,
we are ourselves turning into
a great temptation,
like two parted legs
and what's between them is the perineum—
we've become a kind of dirty fork in the road,
we have two hands, two legs,
two heads,
the twins are our sign,
we're being forced to choose—
some strange result—
some kind of election,
some kind of awful majestic spectacle,
some kind of revolting temptation,
some kind of joke;
fascism: ten years ago fascism was something that students enjoyed
   playing at,
fascism is of course possessed of a powerful aesthetic charge,
and so at the universities there were all sorts of manifestations:
there was a joker named Kuryokhin[13]
a true jester, who happened also to be a talented
musician, a composer who often played his own music;
he played it very well and in the end he played himself out,
and died of cancer at the age of 42;
there were others before him and others after him;
let me try to formulate that again:
"played himself," "played out," "joker";
"shining," "revelation," "romanticism,"

---

13   Sergei Kuryokhin (1954-1996). An avant-garde composer, actor, and rock and jazz pianist from Leningrad. He was also known for his public pranks, or "mystifications," most famously when in May 1991 he went on television to give a long pseudo-scientific demonstration of the fact that Vladimir Lenin was a mushroom. In 1994, not long before his death, he joined Limonov and Dugin's National Bolshevik Party, which at the time was considered fascist by most political observers.

"cancer";
but this wasn't a game,
this was a *revelation*,
everything else was a game,
everything else was a kind of cynical and tragic clowning,
just a series of larger and smaller jokes
(and for many of us
these kinds of revelations
as a result of these lesser or smaller jokes
are inevitable);
a friend of mine once dated
a German and one time
I asked her
how much of the archetypal
image of the German fascist
arouses a masochistic response in a
Slavic girl;
there was a retrospective of Leni Riefenstahl films
in Leningrad some time ago,
and there was some kind of scandal,
many residents were (understandably) against this retrospective;
I sometimes feel like a Leningrad
to which they've brought a Leni Riefenstahl retrospective;
at those moments I understand
why Leningrad
exhausted by drug addiction
major depression
poor health, war,
even its great pre-war poetry
and then cannibalism during the Blockade—
at these moments I understand why Leningrad would need
Leni Riefenstahl;
at all other moments
I do NOT understand
why someone would think

that was a good idea;
right now I know
why I need to remember all this
(and I can't remember how much time has passed—
I think it's been seven years,
but it could be two or three)
in any case,
this was all long ago and really
there's no reason to remember it all,
seven years have passed
who's to blame
who's to blame that
Leni Riefenstahl remained alive
while thousands starved to death in Leningrad;
it's not clear why we need to
think about this now;
tell us about something else,
tell us about the friendship of peoples
tell us about historical reconciliation
and/or cultural exchange,
tell us also
that everyone is alive, and everything's
all right;
God protects all,
though we knew that already,
that's our starting point, our assumption,
but you can still tell us about it,
you'll tell us about it,
and we'll tell those who
need to know;
we'll tell everyone
who knows this already without us
(without you)
and we'll especially tell it to
those for whom it will be

(as everything else is)
just unnecessary
noise, a trap, garbage,
crap,
some kind of sick truism,
which doesn't require any proof
or any commitment
or any other
thought,
we'll pass it on to the rabbit,
the lambs, the goats;
the monkeys, the moles,
we'll tell it to the
crazy cuttlefish,
we'll tell it to every asshole
we meet,
and we'll tell it to
Adrian Frankovsky,
the translator of Sterne and Proust who died during the Blockade,
and he'll approve of our choices,
he'll approve of us,
he'll say:
THIS ISN'T MORAL TERROR
THIS IS AESTHETIC TERROR
(although, why can't we say it to him already?
why, if we're certain that people will hear us
forty or fifty years from now,
can't we be certain
that they'll hear us
FIFTY YEARS AGO?)
I say "I"
but also "we," "ours,"
I don't just speak for myself
but for those
who, like me, can't stand tourism but who, like me,

though not very often,
do get to leave the country
(I can't speak for those
who don't know how and can't leave,
I would never try to speak for those
who don't have the chance to travel),
and so, we believe that
travel is exhausting and
inefficient,
we're tired of looking around,
we're sick of it
(and I'll add from myself
that sometimes a trip to the bathroom
can teach you more than traveling through
every country in—
ah, it doesn't matter),
moving, always moving,
we can't sit here forever,
we can't keep doing this,
we need to move, move,
movement—
this is impossible,
this paralysis,
we need to move,
I close my eyes and see movement, I see large camels, I see
my distant relatives,
I see how my relatives or specially trained nurses
take mortally ill patients through Europe
on wheelchairs;
these are tourists,
most or all of them are tourists,
I see that all tourists
are like these sick people,
I think of what one can do in such situations,
one should anticipate them

the real
the impossible
the never-happened
journey, and not look at real ruins
with lizards crawling on them
not drag one's already
dying body (one's weak, ill-formed, or alternately well-formed and
   slightly foreign body)
through these pleasant evening cities
where everything is frightening,
where everything is good
where everyone drinks,
where so much is drunk,
everything that's not tied down is drunk,
then everything gets aired out,
and then everything ceases to exist—
people will cease to exist—
and a *rupture* will come
and some as yet *nonexistent* people
(like a person vomiting into a sink)
will lean over us, like over a dead crazy cuttlefish (again)
like over boiling cups,
like over crazed vegetables,
and then—
(like over crazed cucumbers)
and so—
just as we, right now, out of stupidity, strangeness, satisfied inertia
want not to be forgotten
(we'd like to leave
tails behind us), we want
to leave something
just as we (when we're gone) will want them to leave US
us
alone, leave US
be, so that the unknown (also, in their way, *in our way*, nonexistent)

people
or not people
concentrations or shadows
some kind of oozing forms
leaving footprints leading toward a fog
wouldn't lean so unceremoniously
over our sinks,
over our raw experimental graves
as over our thin wings
and our transparent light heads
trying to understand
how and what
and when (and what)
happened,
at what point and what exactly,
made us go crazy
and why (why?)
our mechanisms
worked so strongly, but sometimes wrongly,
worked, but sometimes *in the wrong way*,
why they worked, sometimes, more strongly than necessary but in
    the wrong direction,
or somehow wrongly in some other way,
and why people thought so,
and where it went from there,
and what cloud appeared just then,
over a group of unsuspecting monkeys
(and who was paying for this?)
why they wore
small crosses
on their chests
why they sometimes
burned each other's
fingernails
and what they did

and why they entertained themselves as they could
and what, in general, they were thinking
(and why were they defeated)
and what this laughter was;
"where are you going?"
asks the elderly customs agent.
"Rome, I'm doing a reading"
"you're an actor?"
"a poet";
it's late at night.
it's grown dark
and strange
it's
fairly cold, and late,
I'm eating a sandwich,
we'll finally leave soon,
Brest, the Polish border,
and before me
are Polish waitresses
in roadside cafes
who rustle their teeth and tongues
as if nothing had ever happened
(that's just the thing—they rustle them as if nothing had ever
    happened),
then Germany,
Italian girls,
sweet girls,
dark and light,
the most beautiful in the world,
who hug and kiss you at the slightest
provocation
(and forget about you in half an hour)
suggesting that you stay a few more days
in Rome,
Europe after the flood,

part brown and part blond and straw-like, like a field of wheat
    that's been
hoed in straight, geometric lines,
international roadsigns—
and forests standing deep in water
in the south of Germany.

COMMUNIQUÉ [action]

Posted at kirillmedvedev.narod.ru
September 22, 2003

Translation by Keith Gessen

Here's how I see the contemporary cultural situation:

On the one hand, you have a government that is gradually becoming conscious of itself and its cultural priorities, and at the same time noticing, as it will, the cultural figures who are willing to serve these priorities. Or serve the priorities of a new bourgeoisie that is also gradually coming to consciousness of itself and its needs.

On the other hand, you have the idea of "contemporary art," an idea very dear to me, currently existing (at least in its Russian manifestation) as a series of irresponsible infantile games and so-called independent intellectual proclamations—covering the terrain *specifically assigned to such proclamations.*

On the third hand, you have the book market, a clique of half-literate publishers, putting out anything and everything, without any distinctions, hardly managing to slap the price tag on each book in time before shipping it, employing, for commercial gain, the most unprincipled tricks and provocational strategies, flirting with what are to me the most monstrous and disgusting ideologies. You have a brutal scramble for the top literary prizes and endless set-pieces of literary pseudo-events. You have what are in effect a few cultural lobbies waging a nasty and primitive battle for cultural influence; the disgusting speculation of critics and journalists earnestly serving their masters; or other critics, forcing their half-developed, half-conscious cultural viewpoints down their readers' throats, or propagating their cultural or other types of xenophobia and pseudo-religious quasi-fascism.

I find this all very oppressive. I don't want to have even a tangential relationship to a system that has so devalued and cheapened the Word. In such a situation I find it impossible to participate in literary life, to publish even in publications that I find sympathetic, to take advantage of those persons or institutions that are open to me, to develop the literary and poetic community that until now has interested me.

I am interested exclusively in the position of the artist

undertaking a "battle for his art"—which in our own time will mean a battle for his position. The meaning of this is contained not in this or that social function, but, to the contrary, in the ability to see, without distortion by one's social position, without limitations by one's artistic milieu. This is the only position worth fighting for in a time when art becomes increasingly engaged and compromised socially, commercially, and politically.

I refuse to participate in literary projects organized or financed by government or cultural bureaucrats. Only books or magazines put out with one's own labor and one's own money, or published on one's own site on the internet.

I refuse all public readings.

This is not a heroic pose, or "PR" stunt, and it's not an attempt to improve my own publishing prospects. This is a particular, necessary self-limitation. I am convinced that my texts are nothing more nor less than the contemporary poetic mainstream, and that if the mainstream, represented in my person, adopts such a half-underground and, as far as possible, independent position, then, maybe, there will be more honest, uncompromising, and genuinely contemporary art in my country, without ties to the disgustingly revanchist (or, on the other hand, pseudo-liberal) ideological encroachments of the current cultural, financial, and political authorities.

PORNOCRACY [poems]

Selected poems from "Cocks of the Fathers" (*Члены отцов*)
Published at kirillmedvedev.narod.ru
Summer 2004

Translations by Keith Gessen

\\\

I told them to stop publishing me
but they're still publishing me.
what do you think I should do?
fight, or cause a scandal,
or just relax?
should I say:
go ahead, publish me, what do I care,
just don't come to me
asking about it,
which is what you've been doing anyway.
so this is just in case.
in any case everyone is going to have to give up something,
after all only shit is incapable of doing anything about the fact
that it's shit
(and all that remains is to mourn
about it)
I hope that we all have a chance eventually to pay what's due
to pay for everything.
the only ones who'll be able to pay with just themselves
are those who are made of gold or pearls
although we won't be able to tell until later
in retrospect
who was made of what
who they were before
how they were before
and whether they were
GOLD OR PEARLS.
(should I say this?)
I've learned a lot during this time
I've understood a lot.
but there is more to understand.
I live normally now
I listen to the news a lot

more often than I listen to music
I rarely go out
I sit with my baby boy
and edit translations of foreign novels.

— — —

THE GIANT DILDO WAS ATTACHED TO DUDLEY'S
  GROIN
AND ALAN WAS TRYING TO INSERT IT INTO MY BEST
  GIRL.

PORNOCRACY

The French film *Anatomy of Hell*
was released in Russian as *Pornocracy*;
it's not a bad film:
the protagonist is a gay porn star
"with a cock to his knees,"
37 centimeters long—
in his off hours
he starts seeing a woman
who pays him for sex,
and when it's over he starts going crazy—
it was directed by a female director, a feminist;
I asked the Russian distributor:
"why'd you change the title?"
he said: "what do you mean why?"
I said:
"what, *Pornocracy* sells better
than *Hell*?"
he said: "a lot better.
are you surprised?"
I wasn't surprised.

EVERYTHING'S BOUGHT AND PAID FOR,
I thought, out of habit,
in this way sort of grumbling to myself,
knowing already that this grumbling
is the best medicine
for various financial problems
moral complexes
and other forms of spiritual discomfort.
but everything passes—
complexes, traumas, pain,
love, sadism—
relaxation,

suicide—
all of it passes
NOTHING PASSES
NOT EVERYTHING'S BOUGHT AND PAID FOR—
THERE'S STILL A FEW THINGS LEFT.
BUT LET THEM SELL EVERYTHING.
AND THEN PORNOGRAPHY
AND HELL
AND THE CIRCUS—
EVERYTHING WILL BE IN ITS PLACE
EVERYTHING WILL BE BOUGHT,
AND PAID FOR, AT THE RIGHT PRICE,
A PRICE NEITHER TOO LOW,
NOR TOO HIGH
FROM ARTIFICIALLY INDUCED DEMAND.

BIG RUBBER COCK

I saw it every day on the way to school.
I know that's not the best way
to start a poem,
but there's nothing I can do about my memories,
I can't take the rubber cock out of my mind and replace it
with, say, a New Year's tree.
I saw big rubber cocks every day on the way to school—
you could do anything back then—
it was 1991—
and sometimes best friends
buddy-buddy, as the Americans say,
even gave them to each other
as presents
simultaneously
by coincidence,
and it wasn't even a joke
it was natural
a downpayment on eternity
a symbol of one's success and prowess
eternal prowess,
the authorities
couldn't get a grip
on the situation,
they didn't know what to do
about the rubber cocks,
the fairly large rubber cocks,
they hadn't learned to concentrate them in one place,
these cocks were everywhere,
they weren't even manufactured here,
they were imported from America,
which didn't know their true value,
no one knew their value,
in fact no one knew the value of anything,

we all lived like poets—and a poetic fate smelling of resin
(the Russian *rezina* means rubber, that is, synthetic resin,
but there is also in English *rOsin*, hard resin, *kanifol* in Russian,
   but in English like a *rose*
it's a coincidence—rubber rose amber resin rosin)
so this smelly sticky mixture
connected us through the centuries
everything spoken seen and lived
and you can hear the buzz of every murdered nerve ending
every glass of wine from eight years ago
could end up making you vomit
for a very long time—
the imagination is active,
as if a play is on the stage,
and the wine is poured,
your mind is working,
your cigarettes are burning,
your mind is relaxing,
your eyes are narrowing,
the tension is rising
the authorities are rats
but how many more times
will we say about our homeland
our innocent and gentle
if sometimes cruel but in the end beloved homeland:

THIS FUCKING COUNTRY.

\\\

I wrote a haiku:
early in the morning
I buy a condom
from the kiosk.

This really happened—
a Turkish worker was standing
next to me
while the cashier was digging for change.
he was looking at me.
they gave me a condom with a naked woman on it,
thinking, probably, that I was up early and needed to fuck
whereas actually I needed to get a urine sample
from my baby boy.

The doctor suggested
putting a condom on his penis,
securing it in place with a shoelace
tied around his waist,
then waiting.
while the cashier was looking for change
I told this story in my mind, silently, to the Turk,
without stuttering a single time,
and he listened patiently to me, even though he didn't understand,
and when I got to the words "then waiting,"
he even laughed.

But really I should have said:

for the first six months
a child is terribly lonely,
in his entire life
he'll never be as lonely.

there's nothing to be done about this
and it's hard to believe
but it's not something you should try to find out for certain
even if such a thing were possible.

MY FASCISM

[essay]

Published at kirillmedvedev.narod.ru
August 2004

Translation by Keith Gessen and Mark Krotov

My Fascism (a few truths)

Sometimes you hear people described as having "never tasted life." I am one of those people. I look and seem harmless; I'm reasonable, indecisive, relatively well-behaved around others. I don't drink much; I don't sleep around; I haven't used drugs in five years. But I am full of idealism. And that is a lot more dangerous than drugs, alcohol, Satanism, cannibalism, coprophagy, necrophilia. I hope you choose all of the above before you choose my books.

A sickening aesthetic atmosphere has taken hold in our country. The average cultural consciousness is a putrid swamp—half-Soviet, half-bourgeois—in which Pushkin, Dostoevsky, Josef Stalin, the pop star Alla Pugacheva, and Jesus Christ all lie side by side, dead and decomposing. Russia is like a rotten ball, a hideous ball of yarn with a little gold trim on top, but filled with all sorts of trash—trash-food, trash-ideology, trash-culture—and fragments of religion, fragments of "Sovok," and fragments of a dead empire; all of it bulges and sticks out in all directions; the ball rolls and gains speed, ready to shatter into pieces or else crush anyone who gets in its way.

I don't want to draw inane analogies between politics and culture, or provide up-to-the-minute cultural and political argu-ments, but analogies and arguments are inescapable, and so they follow. The parliamentary elections of December 2003 only put the final stamp of reality on tendencies that were already happening in Russian culture and intellectual life at the turn of the century: the nationalists had joined forces with the merely conservative and the outright anti-liberal[14]. What brought them together was their shared hatred of a corrupted '90s-era liberalism and its

---

14   The 2003 Duma elections were a catastrophe for the "democratic" parties that had previously at least made a fair showing in elections. For the first time in the post-Soviet era, neither Yabloko, the more social-democratic liberal party, nor Union of Right Forces, the more business-oriented one, managed to reach the 5% threshold necessary for proportional representation in the State Duma.

manifestations in politics, economics, and art. Our era's intellectual mission now seems pretty limited: the solidification of national values at the expense of all others; a vague but pervasive demand for a single-minded, positivist image of the world; and the introduction of the phony construct of "conservative," "supra-individualist" values, which are opposed to "liberal" consumerism and postmodern relativism.

By the time these forces came together against them, the "liberals" themselves were effectively nonexistent. Liberal journalists and politicians—the "thought-leaders" of the early 1990s—had mostly become ordinary people with ordinary virtues and ordinary vices. They had decided that this was now a *normal country* and they could live how *they* saw fit. (That's probably how it should be, of course, just not in Russia, because Russia never became a "normal country.") Their understanding of politics never progressed beyond perestroika, and after a decade of alienation, privatization, conformism, and even greed, their language was aired out and erased. It was no longer necessary to wait for an election to understand that this was now an empty language: *almost no one* stood behind it any longer.

I write all this because I'm interested in the link between politics and culture.

Dmitry Bykov[15], the poet, prolific essayist, and novelist, has been a leader of the "anti-liberal revolution" of the turn of the century. Over and over he repeats the same idea: that the orgy of permissiveness (embodied in politics for Bykov in the cabal of cheating businessmen and corrupt politicians, and in art by avant-garde poets and modern artists, as well as by contemporary philosophers, whom he describes, not without humor, as "all that derrida") of the sort that took place in the '90s will always be followed—and this time, too—by a bloody political reaction. Bykov wrote a novel, *Orthography*, on the subject; it was based on a spurious but in its

---

15   See the Glossary of Names.

way tantalizing thesis: that there is a direct parallel between the Revolutionary era and the current one. I find this a dangerous idea, not only because it's false, but because it's a falsehood that could become a reality. The intelligentsia's obsession with the past, especially with the beginning of the last century, and its inability to understand, much less accept, a contemporary world that has its own unique laws, is painfully clear. And I write about Bykov because in spite of all his striving for an independent, isolated position, many of the liberal intelligentsia's classic symptoms find clear expression in his work.

The '90s-era Russian liberal intelligentsia had one supreme goal. It wanted to catch up to its Western counterparts, acquiring and digesting the works of postwar Western culture that the Soviet Union had suppressed, and it wanted the modernist heritage from the first half of the Russian century (Akhmatova, Nabokov, etc.) returned to its rightful place. From there it hoped to create a truly "competitive" national culture and ideology. But once it had received what it asked for in the form of its cultural inheritance, the liberal intelligentsia refused to evolve. It continued to debate questions that had been solved long ago, like whether you should consider Malevich's "Black Square" art, and so forth. Superficial changes took place, but regressiveness, provincial ambitions, and a parochial vision of the world ruled the day. What never emerged was a class of *intellectuals*—that is, people who see their duty in a disengaged critique of Authority, in a non-identification with any official discourse. With rare exceptions, the Russian educated class fails to understand this duty to this day.

This intelligentsia's ideal, the poet as private citizen, has not, to my mind, had a convincing embodiment, though many have tried. Joseph Brodsky remains the best example. This was a man who had an enormous influence on the literary scene from his earliest poetic experiments, and was subsequently nominated by a large and in its own way influential intellectual milieu for the poetic representation of its own values. He handled the assignment masterfully, and for his efforts, he received enormous moral—and, as it happens, also material—dividends. The trial against him[16] became one of those events after which, according to every moral and aesthetic law, the country should have shattered into little pieces and buried ninety percent of those who had any connection to the state that had staged it. As far as I'm concerned, a person like that cannot be a private citizen, even if he really wants to be—it's pretentious and hypocritical to pretend otherwise after everything that happened to him, and because of him.

Another tendency in Soviet or anti-Soviet literary engagement is embodied by Vladimir Sorokin. A conceptualist novelist whose early works attempted a violent break with two centuries of "logocentrism" in Russian culture, he presents a very interesting variation on the "private citizen" idea. From the very beginning, Sorokin insisted that he was using his art to resolve exclusively personal problems. In 1998, at the brink of a new phase in his career that transformed him from a cult writer into a fashionable one, he denounced the people who would remain in the underground after he, Sorokin, had come into the light. "Some people," he said, "want to sit in the underground and eat their own shit." It was an interesting choice of words. Sorokin's first novel, *The Norm*, had equated living under the Soviet regime to being forced literally to eat *shit* every day. By bidding his farewell to the underground shit-eaters, Sorokin was announcing that he was no longer in the fight against the real, deeply rooted, inexhaustible shit—the essence of the Russian-Soviet totalitarian unconscious. His subsequent transformation into a trendy plaything of the mass media coincided with the decline of conceptualist artistic principles that had sought to clarify the meaning and mechanisms of art's power over the individual. That critique was embraced by the elite mainstream in the 1990s, but it never entered the Russian cultural consciousness.

---

16   Brodsky was arrested in Leningrad in 1964 and accused of "parasitism" because he did not have a steady job but made a small living as a translator. The trial, after which Brodsky was sentenced to five years' labor in a remote village, became a worldwide cause célèbre and was deeply embarrassing to the authorities. (For more on Brodsky, see the Glossary of Names.)

\\\

Just as culture didn't take advantage of the post-Soviet moment (to develop, to interrogate itself, to change), neither did business. There was no bourgeois revolution, no "rise of the middle class"; instead, we had the creation of a vulgar, vicious, largely ethnic-based clan capitalism. It was Komsomol activists who taught the new generation about contemporary values: careerism, success, drive, the "quick buck," etc. These men told the young: "It's best not to work at all, but if you must work, make sure you are paid for it well, unlike the losers who work as doctors, miners, teachers. He who has the money also has the power." It's strange now to think that business was once portrayed as the enemy of authority. During the 1990s, big business quietly tried to amass and secure power; now those in power are trying to do the same to big business. During the '90s, it was "commercial structures" that evicted Muscovites from their apartments and shut off their electricity; now it is the government that does it, passing in the process whatever laws it needs.

The rise of criminal capitalism in Russia in the 1990s took its toll on books as well. Toward the end of the decade, the publishing industry experienced a real boom. I'm not sure it was a particularly healthy or thriving industry, but somehow or other publishers were making money from books. This engendered the notion that a book could be an object of consumption. And in this way the anti-literary sentiment of the 1990s acquired, in a sense, an economic foundation. Russian literature-centrism seemed to be a thing of the past.

Around the same time, literature began to develop a more acute sense of politics. Literary critics became more sophisticated in this realm than art critics, who, along with the artists they studied, had previously enjoyed something of a monopoly on the analysis of contemporary life. The same phenomenon took place in literature proper. And so there was a breakthrough: tons of books were being published, including many from the West, but the translation and production of these books was carried out cheaply, as the spirit of economic competition was prioritized over aesthetic concerns. As a result, the concepts of rebellion, marginality, and political incorrectness, much like literature itself, were suddenly on the verge of total devaluation. Whether this is good or bad—whether in general it is good or bad when literature and other kinds of art become objects of merciless "Russian consumption" as though they were any other material commodity, depends on whether one approves of the social/political system that has taken shape in Russia, or not, and whether one believes that art has the power to change it. Either way, the triumph of consumerism eventually begat a backlash, a movement in the opposite direction—toward a more politicized literature. Scandals erupted, lawsuits against authors were filed, and some books were even publicly and symbolically destroyed while others were banned from bookstores. Technically all these bannings and lawsuits came from the authorities, but at the center of them, in my view, was a resurgent sense that literature was a central element of Russian consciousness—a sense that had started to lose its footing in the post-Soviet chaos.

(In general, all this darting back and forth between scorn for Russian logocentrism and profound dependence on it must seem funny to anyone who holds a reasoned, Western view that the whole concept of national identity should be treated with extreme skepticism. What's the point? What good does it do anyone? And is the root of evil in Russian logocentrism? In other words, is logocentrism a compensatory mechanism in the face of irrelevance and ideological stagnation, or is it in fact our only bulwark against the kind of evil that does not utter any words at all and refuses to listen to anyone else's? It's possible that both are the case. Recall, for example, the fate of Russian Conceptualism, which in the process of tearing free from the overpowering mythology of Soviet literary culture developed its own ambitions to power, and achieved for itself influence and wealth.)

Right now the government has begun to take an interest in culture, and before long it may decide that it won't be able to create a national idea without dragging literature into it. I mean, if it bothers to think that long about it. But even now there is talk of creating a government-sponsored system of literary prizes, and of creating a unified writers' union, like in 1932, and so on.

In this way, literature, if it wants to have any kind of special status—whether privileged or shunned, which in some sense comes to the same thing—and therefore any kind of special effect, either needs to hope for help from the authorities in the form of direct repression (like the incarceration of Eduard Limonov), or else it needs to take itself out of the frame of the current cultural and economic paradigm—all the while knowing that these kinds of experiments are often in danger of total failure and collapse.

Here I'd like to move away from global problems and talk for a bit about my own small personal relations with culture and literature. I should say that I'm not urging anyone to do as I have done; I just want to explain my position.

Three years ago I wrote a poem about how I wasn't going to translate anymore, because I didn't want to work for publishers and participate in the formation of a new bourgeois culture. It's not that I was dead set on following this rule, but it turned out that, for a while, I really didn't translate much. It was hard for me to stop translating; I'd considered this my calling. But in my logocentric imagination, it was better to renounce one's gift than to force it to depend on the market. And I still remember how not a single publisher wanted to print my translations of Charles Bukowski's poetry. "POEMS??!!" they'd say. I'd get upset but also understand that this was the way of things. Now Bukowski is well-known in Russia and gets published all the time. A large publisher recently put out a book of his poems, but I felt like I was no longer interested, this was no longer what I was doing. I had a similar experience when the magazine *Afisha* asked me to participate in a photo shoot with other young poets, and I said no. What else could I say? What I should have said is: Why didn't you come earlier, why didn't you come three years ago? *THEN* I WOULD HAVE

SAID YES. WHY ARE YOU SO BAD AT FOLLOWING THE CULTURAL PROCESS? In truth, I don't enjoy any of this, these refusals, but there's nothing I can do—if something is easy to get, you should probably refuse it, but more than that I always feel the dark corners of Moscow tugging at me—even now they still exist, even as they're being destroyed and sterilized, and I need to return to them, to run from the glossy magazines, into those folds of humiliation and failure that I came from, and that have always produced the literature that means the most to me. I'm a child of the Russian intelligentsia, I'm a *person of culture*, and culture for me does not consist of rhymes and motifs, but of legends, of gossip, like a thread winding through the centuries, like a moral (as in the moral of a tale), like air—and that's the only thing worth inheriting (not the "outlines of a poetics" or whatever). This is the only cultural inheritance that interests me. I'd like to be the descendant of Leonid Gubanov, the Moscow poet who was trampled and humiliated and yet never gave in to the Soviet authorities, and of Roald Mandelstam[17], who died in poverty and obscurity. Their voices cry inside me, I want to record an album of their poetry, but I feel like I shouldn't, or can't, if I'm a poet with status who is part of the normalized mainstream.

Once, after performing in a poetry competition in Rome, I remember walking around that city, absolutely happy, a kind of successful poet on tour, half-Bukowski, half-Yevtushenko, a real VIP (and at the same time a child), sipping at a gigantic bottle of beer, which seemed to terrify the woman I was walking with, a young Swiss poet, and I remember thinking—or, no, at the time I couldn't think it, but I felt it—that nothing better than this would ever happen to me, not, anyway, in *this* sense, and so I should probably not do it again. That all this recognition, such as it was, and the fact that I'd *dreamed* of this recognition for so

17 Roald Mandelstam (1932–1961). Son of an American who came to the USSR after the Revolution and was arrested in 1937, became a Leningrad poet and early member of the postwar underground poetry and art scene. No relation to the modernist poet Osip Mandelstam.

long, changed nothing. You can't change the world that way, you can't rise to the next level of existence that way—you can only end up getting something for yourself, feeling like a conqueror for a short time. But your ambitions (my ambitions) won't let you just be another conqueror in this city, in Rome. The people who came into the train station (the poetry competition took place in one of the chambers of the train station), and those reading my poems translated into Italian on the big screen in the waiting room, said that they liked the poems; I traveled there and back by bus, it was a long slow trip through daytime and nighttime Europe—I experienced a complete fugue state on the way—I felt like I could see and understand reality without actually coming into contact with it, I was untouchable, and on the way there and back I wrote a long poem whose reading six months later became my final public appearance as a poet.

I have a website, and I'm very happy that this is where my relations with the literary world end. I think this is a very simple and natural state of affairs. I see in this a kind of purity of genre, like a sonnet or haiku or a strictly organized architectural space. I understand that this is how thousands of poets exist. Many of them are talentless, but some are not, some are gifted, and there are probably those among them who are more gifted than I, but no one knows anything about them. In any case, I'm happy to be like them. And people will say: "You're lying. Those poets are unknown and will die unknown, whereas you, in any case, won't entirely disappear. This is just a game to you." And yet I think that in the end this isn't just a game.

I don't like it when former victims, rebels, and avant-gardists become themselves masters of the culture. Like the actual revolutionaries they once modeled themselves on, they often become undisciplined and brutal masters. This is an old and boring story, as old as the world, one that one would really like to avoid in one's own case.

The thing is that for *worries* such as I have, for qualms such as mine, people IN THIS SYSTEM often receive presents—and I would not like to receive any presents.

Of all the many kinds of artists that I know, the only one I like right now (and I should say that I am not this kind of artist yet myself, but I hope to be) is the artist-monk, who has (like a real monk) no rights, only responsibilities. His responsibility is to pray. That is, God in this instance is the social body, which gives some people the talent to move other people, and gives other people other qualities… and in this context praying consists of living an honest life and creating uncompromising art so as to balance out the amount of dirt with which the rest of the social body is filled— be it a narrow stratum, or your nation, or all of humanity.

And the culture that I see around me is busy with other things— whether good things or bad things, they are things that don't interest me, and so I don't want to have any formal connection to this culture. *Is that so hard to understand?*

I am, of course, exaggerating. I'm forcing reality to fit under my favorite rubric of "it's no good." It's not entirely true; some things are good; there are oases. It's possible, for example, that there's something interesting going on right now in the theater. I know for certain that in poetry at the beginning of this decade there was a surge, which went largely unnoticed within poetry circles, not to mention outside of them, because the world of poetry is still on the whole reactionary, even ideological liberals within it are aesthetically very reactionary. But the surge I'm talking about couldn't help but happen, because tectonic shifts in the Russian language are taking place, there's a very powerful process of rejuvenation, as at the beginning of the 19th century, and many successful experiments were attempted, by which you could easily measure the condition of contemporary Russian and its possibilities. You could even measure the condition and the possibilities of society in general by reading these poems.

The main conflict of this time—for Russia, a very serious one—was the conflict between received ideas of *what* poetry is and what it ought to be (simple and "soulful" versus intellectual and complex; rhyming versus free verse; "spoken" versus written, and so on) as against the idea, until recently foreign to these parts, that poetry is only the maximal expression, via the medium of language, of this or that authentic way of seeing, and that it is precisely this—the degree of its expressiveness—that is the only criterion by which you can determine its quality.

\\\

The problem goes well beyond the boundaries of poetry, and heeding Rimbaud's famous slogan, "Be absolutely contemporary!" (a very simple but also very difficult directive) becomes not just a way for poetry to stay alive, but for Russia as well—in fact, the only way for her to stay alive. The great intellectual mission of the 1990s was the creation of a new national ideology—either in its imperial version, when the center, through the force of violence or through the force of its ideas (or, more likely, both), keeps together a host of different, and often hostile, political entities, or in its democratic version, where different entities come together on the basis of the qualities and values they hold in common. *This* was supposed to be the intellectual heroism of the intelligentsia—to work out, within itself, the ability to understand and accept something outside their own personal "identity." The intelligentsia failed to do this. The political consequences are obvious—we were unable to form an ideology capable of creating a single living organism from various political and ethnic subjects living equally together. And the result was war—in Chechnya, in the streets of our towns and cities, and between the young and the old.

This failure took place in the liberal camp. Meanwhile, much more interesting processes were taking place in conservative circles. There, Alexander Dugin was constructing his empire. On the shards of the old Soviet patriotic discourse he recreated an ideology out of all sorts of different items, some of them alien to the liberal culture, others hateful or simply unknown to it—from the novelist Yuri Mamleev to the anarchist Hakim Bey, from occult noise-music to Russian cosmology, from necrorealism to the rock stars Egor Letov and Shish Bryansky, from the Russian avant-garde of the 1920s to Italian Futurism—politics became a giant blanket onto which Dugin tossed all sorts of interesting *stuff*, from the far right to the far left. Technically speaking, Dugin was a philosopher of "Eurasianism," which holds that Russia has a special messianic mission on earth because it combines within itself elements of both Europe and Asia. But the more important thing about Dugin, at least at first glance, was his wit, his liveliness, his ability to see the deep historical interest of elements of Russian pop culture. Generalizing and synthesizing, combining and placing his own emphases, Dugin was able to create a paradigm that incorporated many different tendencies and people in the Russian cultural and political space, but the main thing about all of them is that they were *alive*. This was in sharp, visceral contrast to the liberal paradigm, where anything dangerous or incomprehensible or even interesting either could not exist at all or could exist only formally, not as itself but rather as an example of the liberalism and tolerance of the liberals.

Dugin's system contains a very serious and dangerous temptation, because it could really go in any number of directions. Once you get through some of the fog of esotericism, you can, for example, discover among its ideas some that are forthrightly racist. And if Russia's current "gray administration" can't really have anything behind it but a gray, middling cultural ideal, then a different sort of administration, one more charismatic, even in a sense more cultured, could find Dugin's idea of a "Eurasian empire," with its ontological certainties and sacred truths, very useful indeed.

\\\

Dugin began to combine the right and the left long before they actually came together at the turn of the century, at which point an empty space appeared where the centrist liberal "norm" used to be, and far leftists merged with an ugly new tendency toward fascism, which expressed itself, for example, in the book business, when either for commercial or branding reasons the nationalist-Stalinist Alexander Prokhanov was published alongside the Marxist Slavoj Žižek, and the novel-manifesto *Skinheads: Russia Awakens* appeared alongside anarchist tracts. (I should say I don't think anything should be banned from publication; I just think everyone should publish their own people.)

The undeniable hero of this particular time was a young Moscow journalist who became famous for his various declarations—first about how he went from being a liberal to joining the "Black Hundreds," and then later how he became a Marxist or something approximating one. Reading him you can see how ambition, the desire to express oneself, and at the same time a need to determine one's ideological position can lead a young man to be prepared, unconsciously, to pick up, formulate, and absolutely sincerely argue for any idea that at the moment serves to feed his own ego[18]. I think I have a pretty good idea of how this works—in fact, in my book, *Incursion*, you can see how a person can become kind of crazy from all the various ideological streams moving through his mind in impossibly quick succession. And I think people like this ought to practice art, inasmuch as this is possible, rather than journalism, because in art the reader or viewer subjects any ideology to a kind of resistance test for believability, whereas with journalism you can poison a great number of people with your ideas before you yourself see that they are false, dangerous, and disgusting.

In any case, this young journalist could easily serve as the

---

18   The journalist in question is Dmitry Olshansky, founder of the lively anti-liberal magazine *Russkaya Zhizn'* (2007-2009). For more on Olshansky see: Keith Gessen, "Russia," *Paper Monument #2*.

prototype for a novel about the ideological confusion of the Russian intelligentsia at the start of the 21st century. After the apolitical 1990s, a time of moral and ethical stagnation, there was a powerful surge in political activity and thought. People my age and younger felt like we had to determine our political positions, at least somewhat. We'd spent the 1990s not really knowing what politics was; we lived outside of it; we never believed it could affect our private lives—we were, you might say, young people in the Western mold, but without their history of having fought for democracy, for their rights, for their freedoms. And now, finally, this Russian generation is realizing something. They can still get irritated by "boring" talk about politics, but they do sometimes feel the need to think about things, and some of them, of us, are trying at least approximately to define our positions.

These are the people who need to develop a new, post-liberal, post-intelligentsia conception of politics, one that at the very least distinguishes between left and right (or between "new left" and "new right," if you want). This is particularly important at a moment when certain political forces are working on an amalgamation of the two, a Frankenstein that becomes especially plausible in light of the fact that the Russian government creates a natural alliance between patriots and leftists in their rejection of its politics. (The situation is not very different in Europe, for example in France, where the need to counter American influence, globalization, etc., partly unites the left and right.) The danger of this kind of left-right synthesis is that the general anger in society can easily be channeled into a xenophobic or other unpleasant direction. Sensing this threat, some left movements have actively moved away from any trace of right-ism; I hope, for example, that Eduard Limonov's National Bolshevik Party, which during the '90s actively employed nationalist and Stalinist rhetoric, is moving in this direction.

The leftward movement is held back by the fear that things might go into reverse, that leftist anger might again erupt to the surface. In reality it's a little hard to imagine this happening;

theoretically, however, it's quite easy to imagine, because the left right now is buoyed by the entire cultural production of the past fifty years, from the Situationist Guy Debord to the avant-garde composer Cornelius Cardew to the leftist philosophers Bourdieu, Badiou, and Žižek, from Subcomandante Marcos, leader of the Zapatista resistance movement, to the Russian-born Israeli anti-Zionist intellectual Israel Shamir—in short, the left has at its disposal practically the entire theoretical arsenal of the intellectual resistance of the past half-century.

This, for Russia, is the legendary "world culture" that the intelligentsia has been pining for all these years. This is that relevant, attractive, occasionally fashionable, but until now unknown, undigested, unlived experience that could, under the right circumstances—under a government that was intelligent and calm—become the basis for the world-view of a new, genuinely contemporary intellectual elite; under worse conditions, under a government serving the lumpen fascistic impulses and economic interests of some small portion of the upper and middle classes, it could become the sort of "world culture" whose lack has led to two revolutions in Russia in the past hundred years.

\\\

You can learn another kind of truth about the relations between literature and politics from the cultural situation in the city of Petersburg. I should say right away that I mean the general atmosphere there, not any of the individual wonderful poets, intellectuals, and musicians who live in that city. Moreover, Petersburg is ultimately a metaphor—a provisional space, run down by time, full of artifacts that history has rejected, fallen out of the way of economic circulation. The atmosphere here is extremely tense. You don't necessarily need to hear on the radio about the periodic neo-nazi street march; it's enough just to attend a literary reading and see how aggressively people react to anything unfamiliar, not to mention anything that's actually alien.

The best pages of Dmitry Bykov's novel *Orthography* are devoted to the so-called "dark people" of Petersburg—the lumpen fanatics, lacking any moral norms, golems whom the authorities, not wishing to get their hands dirty, hire to exterminate people. Right now radicals from both sides are fighting for the allegiance of precisely these people, and they're the ones who inspire fear in liberal centrists. In fact this fear is all that remains of the reasonable, judicious, "cultured," liberal intelligentsia.

Skinheads, one of the major Russian newsmakers of the last year, are a close and very real analog to these "dark people." Watching them you can see the mechanism whereby vague signals are communicated between the "people" and the authorities (in this case, whoever controls the media). The skinheads send out their signals: aggression, aggravation, incomprehension, or just plain boredom. The authorities take them in, then send them back in a slightly blurred, more ambiguous, form. (For example, Putin's recent declaration that "terrorism doesn't have a nationality." A nice, liberal statement for the world press; for those in the know it communicates exactly which "nationality" terrorism "doesn't" have[19].) This is what happens when the authorities don't want to speak clearly and don't want to be spoken of clearly, either.

Many of the best-known art works of our time, as well as some publishing projects, are built on the same coy, phony, and ambiguous message, which has also turned out to be commercially successful, answering as it does the natural demand of the audience for positive values and some salve for the wounds of the collapsed USSR.

A few years ago a group of writers from Petersburg made a big splash when they came to Moscow and, during a reading, announced their opposition to "political correctness." These were writers from the major publishing house in Petersburg; they were developing a conservative, imperial, anti-liberal worldview, and

---

19   That is, a Chechen one.

one of their demands that night was that they be allowed to call "faggots—faggots" and "niggers—niggers." (The commotion this episode caused, because of the writers' mainstream position, showed how much more dangerous well-funded ambition is than unfunded ambition.)[20]

As for faggots and niggers, I think you can call them that if you want, without any permission from me. The Russian language has a very valuable ability to turn "correct" language into something offensive—for example I feel like the word "gay," in Russian, has an insulting formality to it. Whereas—in Russian, at least—both "faggot" and "nigger" are kind of sweet.

But the culture won't let these authors speak directly without first asking for permission.

The most significant figure in the 1990s art world in Petersburg was a man named Timur Novikov. Charismatic, erudite, a sufferer for his art along the lines of Oscar Wilde or Derek Jarman, he was also profoundly nostalgic for "European" and in particular "classical" art. Would Russia become European again, he asked, would it link up with the classical tradition, or would it descend into chaos? He wrote passionate essays worrying that the latter would be the case; that Russia would turn its back on high art and slide into barbarism.

---

20   This was a group called the "Petersburg fundamentalists," authors of the well-regarded publishing house Amphora, which was better known for its publications of 20th century Western classics (Borges, Cortázar, Proust) and contemporary eminences (Philip Roth, Salman Rushdie, Amos Oz). The "fundamentalists," whose most prominent member was the novelist Pavel Kursanov, were part of the anti-liberal revolution that accompanied Putin's rise to power. In addition to their visit to Moscow, one of the fundamentalists' most well-known actions was a letter to Putin urging him to recapture the glory of the Russian Empire by taking over the Bosphorus Strait and the Dardanelles from Turkey. To be fair to the fundamentalists, their next letter to Putin urged him to install a system of pneumatic tubes through Petersburg for government officials to use so that they could stop clogging up the roads with their corteges.

All well and good, in a way, but the art that resulted from this reminded the viewer less of classicism than of fascism. (Novikov himself said: "Aesthetically, Hitler was right.") But it would be wrong, I think, to take all this too seriously. It's doubtful that in our time fascism will still be a cult of everything pseudo-classical, black, shiny, and militarized (even as its essence remains the same: the cult of tradition, irrationalism, anti-intellectualism, elitism, the conspiracy theory, and a reliance on the failing middle class). Everyone has his or her own fascism. My fascism is the fatal inability to understand and accept anything falling outside not only "humanity," but my own personal humanity; it's my attempt to hang on to various ghosts instead of admitting that though we're still filled with the shards of the old culture, we're standing now on bare ground. We don't just not have classical music anymore, or literature, or poetry, we don't even have Duchamp's urinal. In Russia right now we're *all* Frankensteins, pieced together from various dead traditions. The maximum that we have, right now, is air.

\\\

There is no intelligentsia in Russia anymore. There are just fragments, moving around Moscow and the other large and smaller cities, remnants, shards. Some have found positions at the glossy magazines, some have started drinking too much and deteriorating, some vote for Yavlinsky[21], some haven't been able to find work at all. What connects them, if anything? Two Russian-Jewish poets of the 20th century, Mandelstam and Brodsky, who formulated two credos: "I'm not a wolf, there's no wolf in my blood," for Mandelstam, and "I like the thief better than I like the bloodsucker," for Brodsky. (Meaning, respectively, a personal pacifism and a kind of ill-defined unconscious anti-capitalism.)

---

21   Grigory Yavlinsky, liberal economist and politician active throughout the post-Soviet era, founder of the political party Yabloko; in 2003 it failed to clear the 5% threshold for proportional representation in the State Duma, rendering it a party of mostly symbolic protest.

We also know that we should not kill. Beyond that we don't know anything. Except we suspect that even what we do know—that you must not kill—can also be a form of pressure, or a trick; it can even be a way to murder. In the modern world, it turns out, you don't need to kill with your own hands, you don't need to be a "wolf"; all you need to do, sometimes, is agree to a tiny compromise.

The proponents of the liberal-Westernizing model must hope (if they have any hope at all, which is doubtful) for the support of this increasingly bourgeois-fied intelligentsia, which grew accustomed to a level of material comfort in the 1990s and is therefore more inclined to the sort of small compromises that will let them keep it. But the proponents of the imperial-bourgeois model also look to this intelligentsia for support. This is the intelligentsia that, a century ago, the authors of *Vekhi*[22] criticized for their idealism and lack of interest in material things. So things have finally changed.

Since the 1840s, Russian Westernizers have taught that eventually a property-owning middle class would emerge as the bulwark of Russian material well-being, democracy, and bourgeois blossoming. The chief disappointment of recent history is the fact that this new Russian middle class, having finally in a sense emerged, far from being the steel in the back of Russian democracy, has turned out to be a neurotic, consumerist mass, full of social and national xenophobia, aggressively clinging to its privileges, ready to sacrifice more than just freedom. It's a group of people who could easily become the central node not of a bourgeois democracy but a fascistoid capitalism.

A different part of the intelligentsia has found itself cut off from material success, unable, or unwilling, to conquer a place for itself in the new market economy. As a result it was humiliated, cast off,

22 *Vekhi*, or "Landmarks," was a much-discussed collection by seven leading liberal intellectuals published in 1909. Written as a response to the millenarianism that had seized much of the Russian intelligentsia, it would become a cherished document for those who opposed the Bolshevik Revolution.

stripped of its ideals and its reason for being (when it turned out that the best people were the rich and the famous). These people were unnecessary to the liberal-bourgeois Russia of the 1990s, and continue to be unnecessary in the red-brown-bourgeois Russia of the 2000s. These people currently form a very depressed and potentially explosive group—they sometimes fall into aggressive conservatism, or hysterical fundamentalism, or into depressive anti-capitalism. This is all perfectly natural, because the collapse of old values and ideals, and rejection from the new world, is a very difficult experience.

If you look, you can see this happen in the center of Moscow on a daily basis. This really very tiny piece of earth—from the Tretyakov Gallery, say, to Trubnaya Square, say, to Gogol Boulevard—this little triangle of land where 500 years of Russian history are concentrated, is now also the most expensive land in Russia. The intelligentsia, which feels that it has a profound connection to this land, cannot afford—literally does not have the money—to remain here. Let me speak for myself. It's dangerous, difficult, and often demagogic to talk about one's homeland, but sometimes it must be done. I have a homeland, and that homeland is the center of Moscow, just as for some people it's a hillside or part of a forest. And to those who destroy your homeland—by cutting down the forest in which you live or chasing you off a hillside so they can build a luxury hotel—well, you can only wish those people death. I don't wish death on anyone, but the people destroying my homeland, chopping down and burning and "clearing" blocks and houses, are chopping down and burning and "clearing out" my limbs and my organs—and I hate them, and will not forget what they have done.

I would love to have been born in a small country, a tiny country, the entire breadth of which you could cover in one day, and the cities of which you could count on your fingers. But I was not born in a tiny country, I was born in Russia, and I identify myself with Russia—I think that's natural and realistic. And because in the future, in this or that collision between it and other systems and other states, I will continue to identify with Russia, I would like her to represent values that are dear to me: democracy, rather than despotism; truth, rather than violence; freedom, rather than servility and ass-licking; solidarity rather than individualism; talent rather than fakery.

I think the intelligentsia ought not to try to cut itself off in elite oases, or enter the structures of power, whether in the government or the church, or for that matter just become part of the middle class. The intelligentsia has absorbed so many of the good and bad qualities of both cultural and ethnic "Russian"-ness (and to a certain extent has given birth to these qualities), as well as those of the other ethnicities and cultures that have been part of what used to be the Russian Empire, that it could now finally digest all this and produce a vision of a non-ethnic Russianness, the kind that's been dreamt of by Russian thinkers for so long. The intelligentsia has been accused of moralism and a lack of pragmatism, of pretending to occupy a position of moral superiority. But what pretending was there in the recent student protests in Petrozavodsk against the erection of monuments to Andropov[23]? This wasn't moralizing; it was a purely instinctive reaction to the shameless lies and hypocrisies of the authorities.

Not long ago I was talking with a friend about the late '60s and '70s, and she wondered aloud whether, if she'd been around then, she would have known any dissidents. And I said to her, well, I definitely would have known them, and you would have known them through me.

But afterward I thought, No, that's not right. If I'd been around then, I may well have convinced myself that I was just a poet, a private individual who needed to work on his craft, and kept my

---

23   Yuri Andropov (1914–1984). Soviet Ambassador to Hungary during the 1956 invasion; head of the KGB from 1967 to 1982; General Secretary 1982–84. Under Putin, Andropov has enjoyed a renaissance, and in June 2004 a memorial to Andropov was erected in the northern city of Petrozavodsk. A small group of young people who identified themselves as antifascists came to the unveiling and tried to place a wreath at the memorial with the words, "From the victims of the NKVD-KGB-FSB." They were quickly arrested.

distance. Whereas my friend, with her strong, unerring sense of justice and fairness—she would unquestionably have been out on Red Square on August 25, 1968[24].

I am a poet. And we poets do not want to be victims of history, we do not want to be dissidents, the very thought depresses us, we are talented, we are avant-gardists, we want to be that which no one has ever been before. But if you force us to become phantoms, if you turn us into the old ghost of the Russian-Jewish intelligentsia, into superficial men and women, into a trembling and hysterical mass of courageous rats—then it will be we who destroy your government, your empire, your authority, who tear it to shreds. Because we will, once again, tell the truth, and the truth, for you, is the beginning of the end.

We need to do away with this false notion of "literature as private activity." Because poetic language in Russia, even the most refined and individualized, is, sorry to say, far from being your private business. It's a source of healing or a method of oppression, it's a potion that can heal or destroy, and Russia itself is a mewling, pulsating mass, full of mute madness, which needs perpetually to be described. There's no relaxing, for the poet. If you don't give Russia a living language, it will take a dead one, a zombie language, a dead form that pretends to be living, and it'll be your fault. And everything will remain as it's always been.

Here is Pasolini, in his final interview, just hours before his death:

> Refusal has always been the most important gesture. Saints, hermits, intellectuals … history was created by those very

---

24   One of the most notable symbolic protests of the Soviet era. Four days after Soviet tanks entered Prague to crush a democratizing movement there, eight men and woman—several poets, a math teacher, an art critic—went out into Red Square in front of the Kremlin at noon with a small Czechoslovak flag and small banners with slogans including "We are losing our best friends" and "For your freedom and ours." They were quickly arrested; most were sentenced to several years of labor in Siberia.

few who said "no," not by the courtiers and advisers, not by the "gray cardinals." But for a refusal to make sense, it needs to be major, not minor; it needs to be total, rather than on individual points; it needs to be absurd and defy common sense. Eichmann had plenty of common sense. What did he lack? He lacked the ability to say "no" to the main thing right away, when he was still an administrator, an ordinary bureaucrat. Maybe he even said to others around the office: "I don't like that Himmler." Maybe he mumbled it, the way they mumble such things in publishing houses, newspapers, in government groups, on television. And maybe he even spoke out against the fact that some trains only stopped once a day so the prisoners could go to the bathroom, eat some bread, drink some water, when in fact it would have been more sensible to stop a few times. But he never put the brakes on the fascist machine. So you need to ask three questions: what is the "situation"; why does it need to be stopped; and how?

Pasolini was a powerful and successful man who purposefully turned himself into a victim. Some of the things he's most famous for—his homosexuality, his dramatic death—can obscure the work that went on during his entire life, his articles, films, poems, and interviews—in his own person he underwent Marxism and fascism, the revolutionary fires of the 1960s, gentleness and disgust toward his homeland (he once said that he stopped writing poetry and started making films because he no longer wanted to work with his native tongue). He always understood art as an uncompromising critique of power.

In our time I believe there has been one man who reacted fully and originally to the collapse and degradation of the Russian intelligentsia: the poet and artist Alexander Brener. Combining the main traits of the Russian intelligent, the Western intellectual, and the "artist from the Third World"—the pride and sense of historical purpose of the first; the independence of the second; the identification with the oppressed of the third—he turned himself into a ticking, internal time bomb. Finding himself face to face with a situation in which the poetic word had exhausted all its force—in the West naturally, because of new technologies of entertainment and a powerful critique of logocentrism; in Russia unnaturally, because of the violent archaization of the Russian literary language under the Soviets—Brener announced his utter creative impotence in advance and began to practice direct, radical actions. To protest the war in Chechnya he went into Red Square with boxing gloves, to challenge Boris Yeltsin to fight him; to protest the commercialization of Russian revolutionary art he spray-painted a giant green dollar sign on a Malevich in the Stedelijk Museum in Amsterdam, for which he received a six-month sentence in a Dutch jail. In the process of all this he posed, I think, some very, very important questions.

The main justification for the existence of the so-called creative intellectual—his self-involvement, his messiness and laziness and odd hours, his overall ineffectual existence—is his ability to perform a speech-act. And the question now seems to be: Either the word becomes an actual act, or it loses all its force entirely, in which case the intelligentsia will have to "act" in the traditional sense of that term (which, by its very nature, and I say this with myself in mind, it does not want to do), or it ceases to exist entirely. (Which may be a good thing, I don't know.) "The hardest thing of all is to be democratic, under any circumstances," Brener and his partner Barbara Shurz write. "What does this even mean? It's the hardest thing. Not powerful, but not powerless: democratic. Maybe that's not the best word. But we're out of words." And: "The first democratic writer was of course the Marquis de Sade. Gazing into the revolution, into its terror, its cruelty, its unsustainability, Sade understood that people are made up of three fundamental elements: Sex, violence, and helplessness."

> Democratic art teaches that we must never, under any circumstances, put our faith in such things as metaphysics, infinity, technique, progress, evolution, or other abstract categories foisted on us by power. We need constantly to

understand that we are mortal, limited, cruel, selfish, greedy, ignorant beings, but if we try with all our might, we may be able, with all our faults, to approach a very intense form of love, and powerful contact with one another, and genuinely elevated expressions of our thoughts and feelings.

I find it hard to forget the story of Alexander Blok[25], who alone among his friends accepted the October Revolution. For me this story continues to yield ever greater and more complex meanings, to the point where his poetry seems less important than what he did during those years after 1917. Whatever you think of it, his story is very much relevant today; Dmitry Bykov recalled it, too, when he agreed to start working at the same paper as the theoreticians of the new Russian fascism. YES, I'M WITH THEM, as Blok once said about the Bolsheviks to his friend Zinaida Gippius. We think of the anti-liberal and reactionary Blok, his victimhood and his madness, his intoxication with the music, the chaos, that would in the end destroy his world and him—we remember this and project it onto ourselves. YES, WE'RE WITH THEM—with the young Arab men whom well-fed Saudi sheikhs tempt into blowing themselves up so as to get money for their families; with the young Chechen women who are sent to their deaths with promises of paradise by strong and clever men; and with their victims; and with the Palestinians in Israel, chased off their lands; with the Russians in the Baltics, where local authorities have erected a monument to the SS just around the corner from the EU; and with the Russians in Russia, who've been fucked over again by their recently elected officials; with Tajiks in Moscow who get attacked by skinheads and harassed by the police; with the "greens" who fight their doomed fight with those who refuse to give up even a bit of their newfound First World comforts; with the National

---

25 Alexander Blok (1880–1921). The leading poet of his generation, a Symbolist and aristocrat who surprised everyone by celebrating the Bolshevik Revolution (most famously in his narrative poem "The Twelve"). In the disorders accompanying the revolution, Blok's family estate was raided and his library burned. He stopped writing poetry, grew ill, and soon died.

Bolshevik Party, which plays out its cruel circus in the center of Moscow, and is beaten and jailed for it; with ... with all of them, we're with all of them, and we feel no terror at the images of our civilization overrun with whoever it will be—Arabs, Africans, Chinese—because we don't have anything anyway, just the air, and that's how it will remain until we have nothing left to oppose it but our race and those things that are fundamentally unacceptable to us aesthetically: conservatism; nationalism; fundamentalism in all its forms, whether the conservative fetish for "fundamental onto-logical foundations" or the fascist fetish for "blood and soil," or the classical or modernist fetish for "high culture," or a positive identi-fication with the "white" world elite, the "golden billion"—I'd like to oppose all of this with a conscious movement to the left, with a critically digested theory of democracy and internationalism, a reevaluation of many of the political ideas and sympathies we in-herited from liberalism, including the idea that we could rationally understand and change the world; an understanding that politics is involved in every minute of our existence (I don't know what needs to happen before people finally understand this); and finally an understanding of the incredible hard work, the superhuman work of reason that will be required to oppose the waves of irrationalism and violence that are now engulfing the world, and those economic interests that often stand behind them.[26]

---

28   This is especially clear now as I correct this article and there's a new mon-strosity: A group of terrorists has taken over a school in the southern Russian city of Beslan, near Chechnya and Ossetia, with children inside, and have been in there, silent, for two days now, not making any demands and not allowing the children to eat or drink. [On September 1, 2004, a group of militants from Chechnya and Dagestan seized a school in Ossetia (a Russian republic bordering Georgia and Ingushetia, which borders Chechnya) and held the children and teachers hostage, demanding an end to the war in Chechnya and the removal of Russian forces from Chechen territory. On the third day of the crisis, after the militants set off several explosions inside the school, killing many inside it, Russian forces raided the school with tanks, artillery, and even an attack helicopter, killing all but one of the hostage-takers. When the operation ended, almost four hundred people, half of them children, were dead. –Ed.]

It's impossible to express any emotions right now, because there aren't any, or,

The idea of a "democratic art" is very dear to me. Not popular art, or elite art, but an art that tries to remove this opposition. An art that tries to look the horror in the face and live with it; that believes, as existentialism also did, that people are nothing but dirt, that they are nauseating, and yet has faith in them; that demands the strictest possible ethical relation to people and art and life; that tries to justify and improve social existence; that proves that all people, no matter their ethnicity or level of education or what have you, are equal and capable of understanding one another, whereas intellect, talent, and education are given to some of them so that

---

rather, there aren't any words. All I know is that these terrorists constitute a reality that crushes and destroys everything I know, and me also, and proves our total and utter uselessness, turning everything I write into a pathetic masturbatory nothing, a pile of words, and turning me into a pathetic lump, lacking speech, and therefore lacking everything—pity, the ability to pity—just as every one of those terrorists, right now, lacks pity, hatred, courage, insanity, fear, and is only that which words can't describe. Each of them is a victim of words, of discourses—religious, cultural, political, economic—that used them up, that turned them inside out, and left them there, pathetic non-discursive lumps, jerking with ecstasy, with that power and that ecstasy of control that all the humiliated, wordless, and doomed to die (and ready to die) experience when they look at people who fear for their lives. (I said I had no words, and now look at all those words.)

Of course this whole story will lead to another explosion of impotence: xenophobia, insanity, monomania. More and more people will become hysterical, shrieking pieces of meat. Of course we need "reason" now, and the traditional leftist arguments—that the military and diplomatic violence of the "civilized world," of the West, against these people, undertaken in order to ensure the comfort and peace of the West, leads to these reactionary explosions of a totally irrational, wordless monstrosity—these seem so true now as to be totally useless. And it's frightening and sad to see one's own government so powerless and useless. It makes you feel your own powerlessness and uselessness. You want to approach it and pity it somehow, help it, say to it: Don't lie to your people, don't treat them like cattle, don't hire half-men to do your work for you. (The last is something that needs to be said to all governments; right now it needs to be said to those people who hired these terrorists to take over that school.) Sooner or later this story will end, too, only I hope not at the expense of many lives—though some have already been lost—and we'll gradually begin to understand what happened, and even, maybe, will be able to talk about and think about what's already been said. One just hopes that not too many people will have died. [KM (September 2, 2004)]

they can use these to go outside themselves and their class, their social position, religion, nation—and then find and proclaim our commonality and equality, to find the language for this and give it to those who have it not.

\\\

This, for me, is the rebellion of humanism. A contradictory and many-layered process, taking place or ready to take place inside me and near me, around me, in the world and in the state—a situation where several senses of the word "humanism" begin to collide. It's a time when the old European meaning, which gave rise to bourgeois culture and the triumphal figure of the free individual, has collapsed. Unable to withstand the terrible pressures of fascism and Stalinism in the 20th century, it led to dehumanization, alienation, and violence against the environment under late capitalism; to the devaluation of all previous intellectual values and their reversal—they were swallowed by the free market, neutered by the culture of consumption, and cleverly turned into their opposites by the new world order, which had its own ideas about things. Now we live in a time when we've learned that Russian postmodernism can be adapted for fascistoid propaganda, and Western postmodernism can be used just as well for American imperialism; when liberalism has become the basis for a cannibalistic neoliberalism; when the idea of multiculturalism/political correctness/tolerance has served to destroy any—national, cultural, *any*—identity that cannot easily be digested by the American melting pot, or doesn't want to be digested; when the final remains of ethnic identity need to be scraped out of one's unconscious so that they don't poison one's entire organism; when all sorts of insane atavisms, from cultural to racial to religious, are hopping around and demanding a re-vanchist correction; when the Russian Orthodox Church is, once again, discrediting itself with shameful bootlicking, teachings of intolerance, and a thwarted will to power; when culture again and again turns out to be weak and unsustainable, discovering behind difficult forms and magnificent constructions a totally "demo-cratic" weakness, envy, stupidity, greed, vanity, fear, conformism, ambition, which leads to violence and ugliness via nostalgia for past beauty and harmony (even nostalgia for ruins), and, on the other hand, restraining the rebellion of an innocent sincerity and humanity, which, on the other hand, themselves contain a totalitarian potential, critiquing the elegant creations of culture but guarding the "soulful," human, humanistic from the frightful "other," from the mutations of human identity, from future clones and living machines, which don't yet exist in reality but do exist in our subconscious, and therefore require a reevaluation of all the norms—both religious and secular—of "humanism"!

We need a new picture of the world, one that brings closer the rational and emotional, which combines various forms of knowl-edge, from political, economic, scientific, religious, cultural, moral, natural, technical, social, and private, instead of blowing one of these up to dominate all the others. People have a new chance at freedom—emotional, primarily, but physical too—freedom from gender, nationality, from their blood, from hopeless atheism and from the heavy hand of the church. People could, finally, be con-nected just by their shared humanity, a new shared understanding of humanity, which needs to be discovered anew, using something from logocentrism, something from postmodernism, something from straightforward utterance and from direct action, something from poetry and philosophy and psychology and culture and counter-culture—and probably something else, too, that we haven't thought of yet—and attaching this to some thread, probably a thread of noise, of music, that we hear inside us, that connects us to one another and to our possible future.

\\\

The political and cultural situation in Russia makes me fear for the future. That future is getting closer and closer. The hostage sit-uation has ended, terribly: A mountain of lies and a pile of bodies, mostly children's bodies, and many of them Ossetian[27]. There's a chance that the thieves and con men of the '90s, with their earth-bound and understandable desires (for money, sex, airplanes), will be replaced by bloodsuckers, that is, by people WHO DON'T NEED ANY OF THAT, who just want to enjoy power for its own

---

27   Which means that these Ossetian children died so that Russia could feel like a Great Power, still. And now the aftermath: The government, working as it always does with hints and winks, suggests that there's some kind of conspiracy, an external enemy besides a group of confused Chechen terrorists, in other words that the West is somehow behind them, possibly through the CIA. And meanwhile the West is demanding answers and accountability from the Russian side, because the storming of the school was so clumsy and caused so many deaths.

And all of it is lies. Lies and lies. And where it's not lies, it's impossible to prove. Compared to the bodies of those little children, everything is a lie. But the biggest lie of all is that we're dealing with something new and unprecedented and especially vicious and inhumane, that the world is splitting up into barbaric Muslims and civilized Christians. Sixty years ago, for several years, a perfectly enlightened European country very methodically killed just as many children as this *every single day*. A different, enlightened civilization dropped two atomic bombs on large cities—were there no children in them??—and then went through the villages of Vietnam, burning them down and shooting their inhabitants. And these really *were* civilizations, these were the *official armies of democratic countries*, and not an isolated group of drugged-up men and women, which is who these Chechen terrorists were.

Russians in Chechnya also have plenty to remember, about what happened to them in the early 1990s, before the war, and so do Jews in Palestine. So I think we're better off not looking for our friends among these people—obscurantist· Islamic radicals, Bush's imperial America, and our own lying government. It'd be good to find something to connect us other than these people and forces. The nationalists keep talking about the need to consolidate the nation against the fifth column made up of leftists and the intelligentsia. You can see the writing on their foreheads: "Bring back the Terror." But things are different now. When World War II began, everything Stalin had done wrong was cast aside because it was clear who'd invaded and why. Right now nothing is clear, and so the only way to "consolidate" the people and destroy the opposition will be through outright lies and provocations. But even then it won't work. The world is different; even Russia is a little different. If the nationalists go this route it won't lead to a repeat of the coming-together that happened during the war but rather to total collapse, degradation, and civil war. For this not to happen we can hope for a miracle—and we can also, as much as possible, use our heads and think. [KM (September 9, 2004)]

sake: the ability to humiliate, the right to kill, the power to absolve. In this context all the old 20th century wounds of the intelligentsia open up again, the terrorist moment adds more fuel to the fire, and all of this, maybe, is a chance to start from scratch, to determine things for ourselves, once again.

Many really think that something terrible needs to happen. I don't want to predict anything terrible happening, so as to have to start waiting for it to happen, and so I'll just say what I hope for: I hope someday to live in my homeland, with my son Bogdan, and to practice my art, unpoliticized, as an ordinary private citizen.

MANIFESTO ON COPYRIGHT

[action]

Posted at kirillmedvedev.narod.ru
November 30, 2004

Translation by Keith Gessen

I have no copyright to my texts and cannot have any such right.

Nonetheless I forbid the publication of my texts in any anthologies, collections, or other kinds of publications. I consider any such publications a disgusting manipulative action by one or another cultural force.

My texts can be published, whether in Russia or abroad, in any language, ONLY AS A SEPARATE BOOK, collected and edited according to the desires of the publisher, released in a PIRATE EDITION, that is to say, WITHOUT THE PERMISSION OF THE AUTHOR, WITHOUT ANY CONTRACTS OR AGREEMENTS, which must be indicated in all the publication data.

I'm grateful to everyone who's published me until now.

— *Kirill Medvedev*

LOVE, FREEDOM, HONESTY, SOLIDARITY, DEMOCRACY, TOTALITARIANISM

[poems]

Selections from a poem cycle published at kirillmedvedev.narod.ru
April 8, 2005

Translation by Keith Gessen

\\\

I am satisfied—I see, dance, laugh, sing,
As the hugging and loving bed-fellow sleeps at my side through
    the night, and withdraws at the peep of the day with stealthy
    tread.
Leaving me baskets cover'd with white towels swelling the house
    with their plenty,
Shall I postpone my acceptation and realization and scream at
    my eyes,
That they turn from gazing after and down the road,
And forthwith cipher and show me to a cent,
Exactly the value of one and exactly the value of two, and which
    is ahead?

—Walt Whitman, "Song of Myself"

a kiosk, an ice cream
fly by in a light fog,
and a man who once tried to pick me up on the street
walks by with his wife,
this was in the underground passageway next to Kitai-Gorod,
he kept at it a long time, he thought I was yielding,
but I was just waiting for a friend,
also gay, as it happens—
my views on life then were strange—
the man buys his wife and himself ice creams,
different flavors—
it's foggy—
I would look at things a little differently now—
for example here's how I'd look at things from the point of view of death,
like this,
from the point of view of death:

"in the splash of sun,
they lay like the blind—
nothing would have distinguished them from the blind
or from others—
and nothing would have distinguished them from us—
or from the young.
over there,
that's what it's like,
and our days would go by,
each of us
would have sex daily."

\\\

I talked to the girl selling vegetables—
without any problems—
without any remarks—
without any remarks or rudeness
on one side or the other—
without any discussion of who weighed what
or who didn't give the other enough
money.
without any sexual subtext.
flirtatiously,
but without any sexual subtext,
it couldn't be otherwise.
professors or bikers—no,
she likes
the guys who work as janitors at the nearby hospital,
and I like little intellectual girls with sharp tongues.
we talked about this and that,
that's all, and it couldn't have been otherwise.
but if I'd been someone else, and
she'd been someone else,
and someone from the side had seen how this thick warm charge
passed through us;
then we'd both have been swept from our places by this wave
and ripped from our roots,
from our universes,
and at that point, as we spun and circled in sterile passages
seriously, happily,
suspended in a solution of tranquilizers,
already living in a cooling world,
I'd have said to her:
"young girl who sells vegetables from a little stand near the metro,
you should know
you've aged about eight years in the year I've been noticing,

and you were made up like a middle-aged whore,
and what's more you were leaning slightly forward,
so that, with the way your shirt fell, I could see your large breasts,
and I swear to you, those were not the breasts of a twenty-year-old girl,
or however old you were last year;
but I had a thought:
they say that Italian prostitutes used to use semen
as an anti-aging cream,
they would rub it on their chests and faces,
and maybe, I think, if I were to rub
onto your round, puffy, debauched, pretty-girl-next-door face,
all the semen I've rubbed over it in my fantasies,
then maybe you wouldn't be in such a bad spot right now."
but it didn't happen, it couldn't have happened,
because we all live in our illusions, like sheep,
and none of us can really help one another with anything.

\\\

a fair-haired boy asks me for ten rubles in an underground
   passageway
and smiles at me when I give him the ten rubles,
we walk in separate directions—
about twenty minutes later I stand drinking tea at a little table
not far from there,
and looking over I see him.
he's from Riga,
his former lover—either a well-known musician,
or something or other,
was supposed to take him to Paris,
but somehow they lost each other along the way,
now here he is
a little prostitute.
(and at that moment I caught myself
looking at him from that point of view—
a fag for sale,
not for myself,
but for someone else—
and this was something that connected me
to the wrong people,
simply the wrong people.)

— — —

and after all the boy turned out
to be pleasant-looking
instead of beautiful.
what did he want from me?
nothing, really, just ten rubles for tea
(he bought tea with the ten rubles
that he took from me),
to talk for five minutes, ten minutes.

I kept trying to duck away into a bookstore
(we were drinking tea next to a bookstore)
but he wouldn't let me go,
he was trying to tell me something:
come closer—
you were trying to tell me something just now—
I want to whisper something in your ear;
no, closer, a little closer; all right:
poor little boy;
I don't feel sorry for you at all.
I'd feel sorry for you
if you were a girl,
I'd feel sorry for you
if you were some kind of toad,
a little piglet, or a ragged chicken—
but I don't feel sorry for you because you are a rock
a rock-person
with moss growing on you, lying for a million years
under a pale northern sun, and, in the winter,
under a cold northern wind.

\\\

a guy in his nicest clothes
standing next to the entrance to the metro
two girls walk by
they must have laughed—
he kept yelling after them:
girls, what's wrong? what is it? girls? girls?
then loudly, to himself now:
CUNT!

an insecure fop, next to the metro;
there was more life in this scene, of course,
than in a pile of battered books;
but this is a collision of elementary particles,
it's a rubbing-together of fragments;
I'm an elementary particle:
my ambition exceeds
the limits of my "I"—
my awesome ambition,
which already exists as if separately,
without me,
like a soul;
does this contradict
the interests of people who want to hang out
and consume,
with their tiny ambitions?
whereas I want—revolution,
to change the face of everything,
to overthrow everything and everyone—
they want
a petty bourgeois revolution—
whereas I have a gold medal for cowardice,
they have—extreme sports;
they have Chinese massage, whereas I have

narcotics, and a cruel regime (enlightened despotism),
profound powerlessness,
and alienation;
among the icy variety of this consumer paradise,
among the objects covered in sparkles, white, and colorful,
we are happy to find that we have nothing in common, except love,
and where they have love,
I also have love,
I love the two girls
who walked by,
I love the boy
who said "cunt."
BUT WHAT SORT OF LOVE IS THIS?
THAT'S AN INTERESTING QUESTION,
BECAUSE I AM UNABLE TO EXPERIENCE
NORMAL HUMAN LOVE—
THE LOVE OF A MAN AND A WOMAN, FOR EXAMPLE,
I CAN ONLY UNDERSTAND SEXUAL ATTRACTION
AND LOVE FOR ALL MANKIND—
an innocent, self-negating love,
and so I ask someone far away, and also self-negating,
but he doesn't answer—as if he's mute or not there,
and that's how I find out that I'm frigid and insane;
the person who was me will never now be with me…

(meanwhile BEHIND me a line is already forming,
of those whom no one ever loved,
no one ever investigated, no one corrupted, and no one killed)

\\\

teachers who talk too much and young waitresses who don't yet
    know what they're doing,
television announcers,
sleepy, gentle nurses,
and others,
all the others,
wherever you are,
I won't list all of you
how are you?
no, forget it.
I want to talk to you:
do you sense
it happening?
don't you think
that things aren't so bad?
doesn't it seem
that time is growing shorter
and shorter,
almost literally shorter—
that it's being pressed together,
that it's acting strange, somehow,
as if it no longer has room for words,
like it's rejecting or dissolving them,
as if the word
that you are now pronouncing
will later already not sound like anything—everything will be
    transformed
and will land like soup into some kind of emptiness,
so much so that you'll forget its very meaning;
this might happen soon—
you will forget not only the essence of what I wrote above,
but even its noise;
what do you think of all this?

have you even thought about it even once?
has this feeling ever entered you
like a knife into butter?
if so,
will you please tell me about it,
because as for me, it's never entered me that way,
to be honest,
though I've thought about it a lot,
that's how it is with me—
the louder I talk,
the more silent I am within myself,
the more I think—
and when I stop entirely,
then just a few short words
(*politics, religion, death*)
remain,
and I can't think of anything else.
for a long time I wanted
no one to know about me,
and then I wanted
everyone to know about my anonymity
and for everyone to understand this as
their punishment;
now I have love
now I spend a lot of time at home,
even though home is the street,
and my language is the language of the street,
and my friends
are the people who sell used books
on the corner—
just now I cut myself in the kitchen
and I yell: Love
I love my girl
I love my love
I love it so much, as if I'm a young man but already famous

a veteran

who's removing from his body, like a splinter, as if from the fire
ANOTHER'S BODY, ANOTHER'S HEAD, ANOTHER'S
    TONGUE,
and presents this to his organs—to his heart,
to his genitals, to his lips,
and calls this by the words, "I have," "I give,"
"to conjoin," "to fuck," "to screw,"
"HOMELAND-PETER-SASHA,"—"MEAT,"
"Lyuba" or "love,"
teachers who talk too much and young waitresses who don't yet
    know what they're doing,
television announcers,
sleepy, gentle nurses,
commas—,,,,—talking birds;
days;
come to me,
while my lover is at work,
come,
come to me,
while my love is at work
COME COME TO ME
BEFORE AN UNSPEAKABLE FORCE
TEARS US FROM OUR WORLDS
AND REFUSES TO PUT US BACK AGAIN
BEFORE WE'VE BEEN PUSHED INTO THE GUTTERS
OF PATHS NO ONE USES
and while we still represent words—
which means, we haven't yet been torn into commas,
that is, we're still just commas ourselves,
and it's only words that separate us.

ON THE PUBLICATION OF THE BOOK
KIRILL MEDVEDEV: TEXTS PUBLISHED
WITHOUT THE PERMISSION OF THE AUTHOR

[action]

In the fall of 2005, the New Literary Observer (NLO) publishing house put out a collection of Medvedev's writings, *Texts Published Without the Permission of the Author,* including essays, poems, and his "Communiqué," in an attractive, perfect-bound edition, without contacting Medvedev, who posted the following response on his website.

Published at kirillmedvedev.narod.ru
January 10, 2006

Translation by Keith Gessen

The publishing house NLO has put out *Kirill Medvedev: Texts Published Without the Permission of the Author*, thereby realizing the possibility implicit in my "Manifesto on Copyright"—that is, an independent edition without any contracts or agreements with the author.

One can certainly be impressed by the courage of the ultra-liberal NLO, which thus violates one of liberalism's core values, the right to private property, and also puts itself at a certain degree of risk—after all my "Manifesto" is primarily an ethical, not a legal, document.

I think there are two possible interpretations of this event; though contradictory, they are to some extent both correct.

> 1) The naive-positive interpretation, which goes approximately thus: "The power of art defeated the conventions of copyright!"

> 2) The sober-negative interpretation: A large establishment publisher put an end to the pretensions of the poet Medvedev to a particularly marginal-independent-rejected position, letting him know exactly where he stood in the cultural context and once again demonstrating the capacity of the capitalist system to absorb all sorts of ideologically antagonistic tendencies.

It might be worth listing the possible motives of the publishing house:

> 1) A sympathy with the author and then a double wish—to play along with his strategy while also problematizing it.

> 2) A sympathy with the texts and a belief that they should be published regardless of the beliefs of the author.

3) An attempt to use the emotions of the texts and/or their quality as ideological weapons—that is, you leftists may be able to write, but you need a liberal press to publish you, since you have no press of your own.

4) A wish to influence the future path of the author—to get him to "return to literary life," etc.

Presumably it's some combination of all of these, though who knows in what proportions. The level of danger in this or that motive is also not entirely clear. And given that, as I understand it, it was a project of two or three individuals who were doing it pretty much on their own, the subjective (good) factors probably predominated. In any case, it's an opportunity to think a little about copyright.

In our country, the following people or groups have a clear idea about copyright:

1) The supporters of maximally strict copyright, which give the copyright-holder total control of his text (the absurd but at the same time perfectly logical expression of this position was the publisher Vodolei's recent attempt to keep a critic from quoting from its Shakespeare translations).

2) The anarchist supporters of the free circulation of texts and other intellectual property.

Everyone else has a very vague sense of the principles and issues surrounding copyright and tends toward the first or the second position depending on their interests at the time.

In general, the situation in the book business is the same as the situation in the rest of the economy. It relies on oil and gas profits, and it is characterized by big businesses (in this case, publishers) who made their way criminally in the 1990s now lining up to receive their "amnesty," legitimating their profits[28]. The strengthening of copyright law is a kind of analog to this amnesty, even though the large industrial corporations still don't shy away from the criminal methods of the 1990s (not paying royalties; fooling authors; messing with the text; running off extra copies without telling anyone; disappearing). In general, though, the loyal oligarchic money that is spent to pass such laws is increasingly interested in stability, with copyright as with everything else.

It's also well-known that the normalization of copyright in Russia is being demanded by the World Trade Organization, whose potential inclusion of Russia will have very doleful results for the people of Russia, as it has had for many peoples in the Third World. I don't know how the publishing house NLO feels about it, but I personally have a very negative view of Russia's possible entry into the WTO.

In my opinion, our local criminal bourgeoisie and the transnational bourgeoisie deserve one another. They both know how to use force when necessary, and how, when necessary, to pass the laws they want. But the general banditry of contemporary Russian society, its contempt for the law and for people in general, should not make the Russian artist long for the laws of the Western art and book business, with the help of which the capitalist system keeps itself going. Copyright is one such law.

This story also has another, more private, I'd say ethical side.

The question of copyright is partly connected to the argument, which continues unabated in poetic circles, of what is most important: the text, the author, or the author's "project." Those who say the text is most important are those who often get the most

---

28 Not long after assuming the Presidency in 2000, Vladimir Putin convened a meeting with the major oligarchs and offered them a deal: if they would stay out of politics, Putin's government would not investigate the ways in which various oligarchs had gained their riches. This came to be thought of as an "amnesty." Most oligarchs fell in line; the most notable holdout was Mikhail Khodorkovsky, who remained politically active and was arrested in October 2003.

dividends from their texts, or are otherwise involved, one way or another, with literary politics. This is strange. I for one identify with my texts completely; I consider them the expression of my own—conscious, semi-conscious, or unconscious—emotions and ideas. (This is why I can't accept the principle of anonymity, even though I find it attractive. Rejecting not only copyright but authorship itself would, I think, be dishonest with regard to my self.)

I think the idea of separating the author from his text makes a certain amount of sense in the context of the internet-author, who really doesn't have a name or a body—that is, in a situation when only the author knows of his connection to the text. In all other instances the idea of separating the author from his text has either a metaphysical underpinning (the text is an expression of certain supra-individual essences) or a deconstructivist one (the text is immediately an object of interpretation and manipulation, outside the power of the author). And both these tendencies deserve very strong suspicion on our part, having either been exhausted or seriously discredited for the current cultural moment. The author cannot entirely control the interpretation of his text (in this sense the text is indeed independent), but the author can influence the context of its interpretation—by his non-textual activity he can support, expand, vary, or try to cancel the connection that he initially has with the text (as its author).

For me personally, NLO's gesture has brought to the surface and accelerated the conflict between two ambitions—the natural wish to be read and understood, on the one hand, and on the other the wish not to be involved with the conditions that in many ways have allowed me, thus far, to be read and understood. The conflict between these ambitions and the possibilities for it to be resolved continue to trouble me.

I know perfectly well that 90 percent of the people who care about poetry do not care about any of this—what difference does it make where the poems are published and on whose dime and who owns the printing plant; all that matters is whether they're good poems, right? Right, right. And that's exactly why I'd like to say that if this episode elicits even a tiny amount of thinking about the subjects raised above, I will consider it a success for me—regardless of how well, or badly, or not at all, it reflects on the reading of my texts, their author, or his project.

THE END OF THE CEASEFIRE
(THE END OF THE OBJECTIVIST SCHOOL?)

[poem]

Posted at kirillmedvedev.narod.ru
August 9, 2005

Translation by Keith Gessen (with Isabel Lane)

On February 23, 2005, the first day
after the end of the ceasefire[29],
I was riding the metro and noticed a man
watching me very carefully.
"…and the Russians will understand,"
the Chechen rebels had recently said.
more precisely, they'd said:
"and the Russians will understand that this was
a *real* ceasefire."

this statement made no impression on me at the time,
I wouldn't even have remembered,
but apparently it made a strong impression on this man,
he's clearly nervous, looking at me,

I haven't shaved, I'm standing here
with a hand on my belt,
smiling crazily to myself about something,
thinking of something.

the train sits at the station for a while,
as if giving the man a chance to save himself.

finally, glancing at me one last time,
he jumps out.

---

29   The Second Chechen War began in August 1999 and resulted in the brutal
re-invasion of Chechnya by Russian forces. By May 2000, the popularly elected
government led by Aslan Maskhadov was deposed and a pro-Russian government
set up in its place. The war continued, however, as the former government took
to the hills. As Medvedev indicates in "My Fascism," the years 2002-2004 saw
a series of ghastly partisan attacks on Russian territory, including the seizure of
a theater in central Moscow and a school in Beslan, in southern Russia. In early
2005, that is, just a few months after Beslan, Maskhadov announced a unilateral
ceasefire as a "gesture of goodwill." The ceasefire was to run out on February 22,
the day before the anniversary of Stalin's deportation of the Chechen population
to Kazakhstan in 1944.

he runs to the middle of the platform and freezes there.

he's not crazy
to the contrary, he's probably perfectly sane,
everyone should be as crazy as this guy,
and everyone is,
it's just that our minds are weak.
you never know
what will make an impression on someone.
you can't do anything about a weak mind
you can't do anything about your own mind,
much less someone else's.
now I'm in Berlin, where I'm waiting for a late tram with a friend,
who's telling me about a scene
he witnessed the last time he took a late tram in Berlin:

a man eating a slice of pizza gets on the tram,
and the driver growls at him to get out,
because you can't eat pizza on the tram.
the man gets out and starts skipping down the rails in front of the
    tram,
eating his slice of pizza.

the driver is furious.
the man finishes his pizza and gets back on the tram.

meanwhile some drunk hippie with long hair
is on the tram,
and a skinhead's walking by him,
the hippie says,
"hey-hey, that's a good haircut, man,
I want one like it."
"I can give you one," answers the skinhead,
"I even have my clippers with me."

I laugh,
I love this scene.

Anisa left earlier today,
and I'm leaving tomorrow.
but for now me and my friend from Berlin,
the one we stayed with,
are still out.

first we sat across from the club
where Bowie and Iggy Pop played in the '70s,
drank some beers we bought from some Turks,
and then drank wine with two other friends,
then left them and visited
a Russian singer we know;

the cab driver who drove us there,
spoke a little Russian,
and, letting us out, said:
"so now we hit the whorehouses?"
I like this.
I like that we're walking around Berlin.

my friend understands me pretty well,
I remember reading somewhere:
"I have three friends who always understand me.
one lives in London, another in Ljubljana, a third in…"

that's how it goes,
and it's good.
no one should understand a man
in his own country.
for a prophet his homeland is enough,
what more does he need?
right?

you understand?

the people who understand should be so far away
that you can't talk to them on your cell phone or on email,
or over a regular phone,
otherwise what could force a person
to travel so far,
what would force him to pay
these miserable embassies,
and tourist companies, and trains?
nothing could.

rocks, the sea, houses, cathedrals, women?

no.

the cab driver had this accent, and he said,
"so now we hit the whorehouses?"

the singer we were visiting lives in a neighborhood of gay bordellos.

yesterday,
Anisa and I
were standing in line at the exhibit of a fashionable young artist

in front of us in line
stood two gay men

both were tall,
and looked down on us
when we answered some question of theirs
in our crude English.

two good-looking men
they probably work in television

or in some other media
attend exhibits
and probably consider themselves bohemians,
or rather, define themselves by this term,
which they inherited
from the cursed, talentless, nameless,
from the dispossessed,
who had nothing in this world
except this intoxicating romantic definition
which they in turn got from the Gypsies.

and what place, incidentally, do gay people have in the
    contemporary world?
mostly these are well-paid graphic designers and advertising men;
like Jews, they've mostly forgotten about their curse and their
    rebellion,
and only remember their identity

when there's some chance to profit
from it.

I like them (I'm biased)

I was rarely objective before
and now I'm not objective at all.

and the conclusion is this:
too much sympathy is dangerous,
it's just dumb,
it's unnecessary—
it's an unnecessary anachronism,
it's time to treat all representatives of minorities
as regular people
and that's all.
all problems, complaints, and misunderstandings

come from too much sympathy.

you can't treat everyone like they're your relative
Jews, gays, millionaires
Israel and the USA.

which is something we should have realized
long ago.

on the other hand I say all this
as if I'm the member of some majority,
which is strange.

I came to Berlin on money
earned by my girlfriend.
this whole tram stop is covered in stickers.
they say, "don't make space
for Nazis and anti-Semites."

I should take one down
and keep it.

the objectivist school, I'm thinking,
the objectivist school.
Or, rather, "objectivism."

this was a direction in
American poetry.
it had the following characteristics:
leftism, a concept of "sincerity,"
a Jewish identity.

that's interesting, I think.

how do these qualities

give birth to
an unbiased view of an object?

(Aside from the US, the objective movement in one form or
    another
developed in many countries of the developed world,
and recently, for example,
in Latvia, where the particular European quiet and calm,
the prosperity of a small space,
and the relative unity of society,
could give birth, until recently, to a particularly restrained
view of the world,
one that appeared to rise above political and social differences.)

across from me an old woman is talking to an old man riding next
    to me.
it's May 1, May Day,
she's holding a roll of papers, it looks a lot
like a rolled-up poster or sign.
suddenly she starts asking everyone for a tissue and
I give her a tissue.
then I see that a guy sitting next to her is throwing up on the floor
and she gives him the tissue.
the guy mumbles, "Thanks, grandma,"
and wipes himself off,
then gets off the train,
an old man sits down in his seat
next to the old woman.
a woman sits down next to me
with a burning icon-lamp,
she squeezes it in front of her like a little chick.

space squeezes space place time reality.
my friend accompanied me to the train station
and we talked of this and that.

he didn't want me
to rush back into the Russian panopticon.
a man on the platform between stations in the metro in Moscow
screams
pressing his face to the wall
covering his ears with his hands
like a man struck deaf.
what is it?
his heart?
he's gone crazy?
he's lost it?
it's a terrorist attack?
his face and a portion of the wall
are covered in the purple light
of a cell phone.

this old lady doesn't get off at Teatralnaya.
is she going to the meeting of the democratic opposition
at Lubyanka?
whereas I'm going to the communist meeting on Teatralnaya.
I want to see
who there's more of:
leftist-internationalists or Stalinist-nationalist-anti-Semites.

but she's going who knows where.
objectivism is when the author pins down events,

and sometimes I think: how large a budget would you need to be
    truly
objective?
how large a budget would your cameraman need
to record things sincerely—beautifully and without bias,
but not in such a way that one would ask: *why are we here and*
    alone?
where is our director, costume designer, producer?

and why?
the men carry their beers,
reality jumps,
falls away.
it disappears,
and no curse is laid upon anyone now at birth
because of their religion
or their method of fucking
or their citizenship.
it's not given to anyone,
and there's no reality in Berlin,
or in France, or in the USA,
or in the Baltics—there's just the Russian language,
this fucked-up honest organism;
when you want to say something too correctly
it always comes out sounding false.
and so, there's no reality in the Baltics,
just like everywhere else,
and there's no reality in Russia,
there's just the remains of the male, the female, the fathers,
and Jews, gays, Muslims,
the intelligentsia, the Gestapo, the Russians,
just like everywhere—the waste products,
these pathetic remnants,
nonsense,
soup, waste,
this is the Great Dreg,
the mighty stagnation
the remnants of idenitity
like the last remains
that need to be scraped out
the way you scrape out the rest of the fetus
after an abortion,
but

I'm for purity
and I'm for every individual identity
but it's something you need to fight for,
like for a clear writing style, like for lies,
and it won't give you anything but awful untruth
or the opportunity to die in battle, or live alone,
or die alone or among many others,
yes,
in any case, without any profit,
with nothing left but blind worrisome confusion
only wild blood flooding and clearing the brain,
and in any case there's no objectivity,
it's impossible to simply look at it,
and you won't touch reality,
because reality is cursed and guilty,
and you have to fight for it, just as you have to fight for being
    cursed
and being untouchable,
losing blood, sight, sincerity,
your Jewish or any other identity.
that's all I wanted to say.
no—actually—one more thing, an addendum. New Year's day—
"Lovers imprisoned
in the half-transparent fruits of an enormous vineyard"
(V. Krivulin)—
lovers imprisoned in a transparent cocoon
made up of wine vapors
she's around thirty
he's five years older
and by the exhaustion of their movements
and by the extent to which they're used to this state
you can tell they've been drunk
for a while now.
they probably brought in the New Year together
or in a small group,

and everyone ate a lot, and drank a lot,
and then slept a little,
or maybe didn't sleep at all,
and now they've decided to start up again.
they pay for a bottle of vodka, and something else, some sardines,
but they forgot their sausages!
we hand them to them,
and their cocoon pops,
it melts,
and at that moment they meet us
there's a transgression, a crossing of boundaries,
a collision,
like a bomb in the metro,
and we find ourselves in our uneven, jumpy world,
our child was just crying excitedly,
as we passed the groceries,
and yet these sausages,
these specific sausages or hot dogs,
became that boundary,
this border post,
where these two worlds, if you like, met,
and then they left.
but we'll meet them again,
or someone like them,
when the New Year ends,
because they'll find themselves in our world,
in our jumpy happy hell,
and no appearances or amount of fairness
or unfairness,
no objectivist school
or even objective truth

will get in the way.

DMITRY KUZMIN: AN ESSAY-MEMOIR

[essay]

Published at kirillmedvedev.narod.ru
March 2006

For more on Kuzmin, see the glossary in the back of this book.

Translation by Cory Merrill and Keith Gessen

Dmitry Kuzmin: the well-known publisher, editor of anthologies, and engineer of literary life is also well-known, though less distinguished, as a poet, critic, and translator. I want to write about him because I think he is one of the most important and interesting figures in contemporary Russian culture, and because over the course of a decade I have observed his work—both from the outside and from within, as his colleague.

We were introduced by the poet Danila Davydov at the beginning of 1998. Davydov and I were studying at the Gorky Literary Institute; Davydov had been working for a while on one of Kuzmin's many projects, the paper *Moscow Literary Life*, which on a monthly basis published firsthand reports about practically every literary event in Moscow. After reading one of my essays in *Russian Journal*, Kuzmin invited Davydov and me to a reading at Avtornik, on Maly Kiselny Alley. Afterward the three of us left "to drink kefir," as Kuzmin put it, at a bar above the arch that leads to the Kuznetsky Bridge metro. Kuzmin actually did drink kefir, which he then had to share with Danila and me, since we didn't have any money. Over kefir Kuzmin explained to me his vision of the paper and his work in general.

So I began to go to literary readings (mostly poetry) and write them up. I adopted the thinking of the paper pretty quickly, in truth I was close to it already. The idea was to evaluate poets not according to one's vague and subjective emotions, but to the context from which they'd emerged; to insist on the author's right to innovate; and to criticize everything traditional and passé. Innovation was the key. If Kuzmin saw even the slightest inkling of it in a poet, he drew him in, either by publishing him in his annual literary anthology, *Vavilon*, or encouraging him in some other way—basically, one way or another, he kept an eye on him. He proceeded according to what he called a general "ecological" approach—the creation of a large meta-space (an ecology of poetry), which was to include the most varied but at the same time interdependent poetics, consisting of all the authors working in some new vein, regardless of the scale or even quality of that work. The idea was that over time, with the success of liberal reforms and the general emancipation of the population, this poetic space would become a major cultural phenomenon, and play an important and positive role in Russian culture. In the meantime, Kuzmin would reinvent the Russian poetic sphere. He published papers, magazines, and dozens of small books; he hosted events, engaged in polemics, organized conferences. Not long after we started working together, he made one of this savviest moves: he decided to make the *Vavilon* poetry anthology a web-based publication, dramatically expanding both its reach, its frequency, and its archival potential. In this, as in so much else, he was so far ahead of the rest of the literary field as to be playing some different game entirely.

And so I went to readings and wrote my reports. I can't say that Kuzmin and I became friends—we had strictly professional, or rather, collegial relations. I shared his central preoccupations and believed that we were doing something important and progressive. When I began to write my own poems, Kuzmin took to them with great interest—sincerely, as far as I can tell—and really saw something in me, I think, with all his heart. He began to publish and promote me. I, in turn, followed him with great interest and, in general, sympathy, as a man, poet, and activist. Kuzmin was, quite clearly, a very powerful irritant to the average Russian cultural (un) consciousness. He possessed and possesses qualities that in discrete doses are more or less tolerable, but at his level of concentration produce a phenomenal effect.

What are these qualities? He is, in no particular order, a homosexual; a Jew; a libertine; he doesn't drink or smoke, has an exceptional work ethic, and a personal poetics. It's his work ethic that has allowed him to achieve so much. Prize juries, magazine editors, and festival organizers all want to deal with a more or less finished product. They therefore inevitably gravitate toward familiar names and recommendations. To find a new and controversial author in the slush pile and take responsibility for his publication: this is incredibly difficult. And there's no question that all editors in all times and places simply throw away a large portion of submitted manuscripts without so much as a glance. Isn't this the true explanation for the conservatism of Russian literature, and of literature in general? Kuzmin, by dint of his extreme curiosity and interest in others' work, is able to dig through huge masses of texts in order to find the occasional diamond in the rough. As a result he simply outcompetes the editors of the print literary journals with their conformism and delayed reactions. Kuzmin is also an indispensable figure in the organization and hosting of literary events, festivals, and the like. He does this work with real flare. He loves the visibility, to be sure; but it's also the case that organizing a literary conference is as important and pleasurable to him as digging through the submissions of young unknowns. This is important not only on a personal, but also on a general cultural level. He once explained it like this: People come to him with some idea for an event, out of which they want some kind of gain, but at which they do not particularly want to work. Kuzmin happily accepts, does the work of selection and organization, and, while his "customers" get the short-term benefit, whether it's money or prestige or whatever, in the long-term it's Kuzmin who wins. He and his project. This is great; and it's also entirely fair. He is disrupting, in a way, the entire literary (and social) system whereby the higher you climb, the further you get from the dirty work, and the more you profit at the expense of others. Kuzmin in that respect is a rare type.

Starting out in the early '90s, Kuzmin understood right away that you had to be independent, to build your own organization from the ground up. That was a very important thing to realize back then. But of course there was a catch. In order to attract attention to your unknown organization and its obscure writers, you had to get well-known writers and organizations involved. You needed to create an autonomous institution, yes, but make it so that eventually other, more established institutions were (in a good sense) dependent on it. Kuzmin did all this with his usual scruples and taste; he never lined up the usual suspects. He printed previously unprintable classics from the late Soviet underground (Sapgir[30], Aizenberg[31], and others had their first "official" appearance in Kuzmin's *Vavilon*), and published these alongside younger poets just starting out. Thus his project eventually broadened, and new poets emerged. He published a multitude of authors no one else would have taken on. He truly, sincerely believed in all of them as writers, never publishing anyone, for example, out of charity or friendship. (This was, by the way, one of the nastier aspects of the Soviet system, the fact that editors so often published their friends. This is pure feudalism. Of course it goes on everywhere and always, but in Soviet times it passed all bounds and infected everything.) Faced with various temptations, Kuzmin stuck to his principles; these were, ultimately, the true calling card of his entire project.

Its other aspects were provocation and systemization. Kuzmin excelled at giving names to poetics and movements, slotting them into categories, finding antecedents for them in Russian literary history. This may sound boring or academic, but in fact it is immensely useful, it gave young poets an immediate pedigree and helped readers and critics orient themselves in the new literary space. At the same time, Kuzmin was oppositional. What did he oppose? It would have been disingenuous for him to oppose the post-Soviet regime that made his project possible (and, as we'll see, he would not have wanted to in any case), and so Kuzmin's chosen target of scorn was the "Soviet." Official Soviet culture was anathema to Kuzmin, and he frequently associated himself with the Soviet underground, assuming for himself a deep split and rupture with those (disappearing) authorities. There was

---

30   Genrikh Sapgir (1928–1999). A poet associated with the non-conformist Lianozovo school of artists and writers, which included the painters Oscar Rabine, Lev Kropivnitsky, and Lidia Masterkova, as well as the poets Vsevolod Nekrasov, Yan Satunovsky, Igor Kholin, and (briefly) Eduard Limonov.

31   Mikhail Aizenberg (1948–). A poet and critic who formulated the aesthetics of the unofficial poets around Moscow Conceptualism in the almanac *Lichnoe Delo* (1991). He has written several books of poems and many essays on contemporary Russian poetry.

always something fraught about Kuzmin's conflict with the Soviet; Kuzmin himself was in many ways a product of the Soviet intelligentsia—his grandmother, for example, was the Soviet translator of such beloved classics as *The Little Prince* and *To Kill a Mockingbird*. It's not clear that had Kuzmin been born twenty years earlier, he would have found himself in the underground; it's possible he would have been the editor of some more or less progressive journal. And he would have used his power to fight for interesting, worthy authors. (Now that I've written this, I start to doubt it. In any case, had Kuzmin been a member of that culture, the culture would have had to be different. Otherwise he would have been thrown out of it. Or maybe not? I don't know.) Either way, Kuzmin's systematizing and provoking and anti-Soviet tendencies sometimes find themselves in direct conflict. He has argued, for example, that the popular notion of a chaotic or even anarchic underground is false, that in fact anti-Soviet literature was an ordered system just like any other. But this is a quixotic point to make. To be sure there were networks and nodes in Soviet underground culture, and figures around whom much revolved, but the only place where it is anything like a real system is in the imagination of Western Slavists and in Kuzmin's head. Also, in the archives of the KGB.

\\\

The most important thing about a poem for Kuzmin is whether it's new. He tends to assume that everyone knows what is meant by this, but in fact no one does. What makes a poem new? How can you tell? There are its formal qualities, to be sure, but the number of formal qualities a poem can have is limited; whereas the potential for innovation must be unlimited. So there are other qualities, too, that can make a poem new.

In my experience, the mark of novelty is less formal than social—that is to say, it is an intersection of what is on the page with what is off of it.

When I read a poet who is truly new, I find myself seeing not only the words on the page but, behind the page as it were, a *new* group of people. This is the poet's imagined audience, to some extent; every poet has one; the new poet is one who in the process of imagining this audience also brings it into being. These aren't just his friends or people who could be his friends; they are people who *could be his readers*, who relate to what he's put down and the way he's put it down. They won't all necessarily come into contact with his poetry, in fact most of them won't. But in the work of a truly new poet these people suddenly come into view.

To take one example, there is a poet named Stanislav Lvovsky, whom I have long loved and whom Kuzmin also loves, often citing him, for various reasons, as an exemplary Vavilon poet. In his poetry, Lvovsky describes the social, cultural, and emotional lives of a particular social stratum—the young Moscow Russian-Jewish intelligentsia, aged about 25 to 40, which finds itself working in various quasi-cultural spheres—advertising, design, journalism, TV, and so on. Lvovsky began to ply this terrain in the mid-1990s, just as this particular stratum was first coming into being in our country. He did not, in other words, start writing his poems in response to a demand that already existed, but rather formed alongside this group and its demand for self-expression. He wrote about the problems of money, and freedom, and up-to-the-minute technology, problems that his (and my) parents' generation could only really dream about. Here he is, for example, on what it's like to be the first generation of Russians in nearly a century that is able to travel widely, freely—and lose touch with one another:

> I'm sitting in the Cafe-Zen
> near the Belarus train station;
> it's got see-through windows
> opening on the square
> near the trains for Kursk and Orel.
> [...]
> It's our war with ourselves
> that's brought us here.

Look at the traffic.
This is the only place in Moscow
with such traffic.
Where you literally cannot breathe.
Where the diesel spills
into rivers that float down toward a sea
that isn't there.
Where the fires also float
in the heavy current,
and this is the storm.
The train for Berlin leaves from here.
Samarina lived in Berlin.
You should remember her.
(I don't know what to do
about this habit of writing
about the living,
although to be perfectly honest
I've long since ceased thinking it was a problem
because of course
I write about them
as they live inside me,
rather than as they really are.)
Then she turned up somewhere
in New Haven.
These American
names,
they're straight out of the Bible.
New Sky.
New Land.
We lost touch,
as usual. […]

Lvovsky is a good poet. But how do I know he's an *original* poet, a *new* poet? It's because I know that I can gather a group of people together in a room in Moscow right now, and this group will either know and like Lvovsky's poetry already, or they will like it as soon as they hear it. And what's more, their affection for Lvovsky's poetry will be the *only thing* they have in common. There is a sense in which this group did not exist previously; now it exists; and Lvovsky may be said to have created it. A decade ago it would have been hard to see the outlines of this group, or say with certainty that it was there. Now there's no question. And in fact to some extent Lvovsky is no longer as interesting a poet as he was, because the group he describes, and speaks for, and once brought into being, is now a fairly familiar group. The point is, when Lvovsky was first writing those poems, it wasn't. At that time, Lvovsky managed to organize the nascent group of Moscow yuppies along different lines, in some kind of different way, from the strictly professional or social or geographic way in which they were otherwise organized. And at that time therefore as a poet, he was new, and his poetry was, objectively, original.

I apologize to anyone who finds this approach to poetry too strictly sociological, not to say crude. And yet you cannot under-stand the significance of Kuzmin—and the failure of Kuzmin—if you do not also appreciate the extent to which poetry always comes from among a certain group of people; and addresses certain other groups of people; and eventually organizes and inspires the activi-ties of those people, or fails to.

\\\

Kuzmin's poems need to be discussed separately.

When he was young, and apparently up until the mid-'90s, Kuzmin wrote traditional poems: that is to say they rhymed. As far as I know, these poems weren't well-received. At least I never saw them published anywhere. I don't know how Kuzmin feels about this—he may well feel it's for the best. In any case, eventu-ally he started to write a kind of realistic free verse, in the spirit, as he said, of "the objectivist school." These were well-constructed texts, sometimes merely elegant and nice, at other times more provocative. They could shock, and sometimes do shock, the average reader, should he suddenly come upon them somewhere. Nevertheless, Kuzmin published them sparingly, following one of his firm principles—never to use Vavilon to promote his own work.

In my opinion, Kuzmin was a good poet. He has described himself as a second-rate poet, and, what's more, has listed the characteristics of second-rate poetry and pointed out how they fit his own work. For some, it may seem old-fashioned for a poet to speak of himself in this way. In my opinion, Kuzmin did right. Moreover, he was right. He was a good poet even if he was not the best poet. He mastered a poetics that is unique for our country even if it's not a discovery on a global scale.

The subject of his poems is the relatively stable and happy life of a gay man in a disturbing, violent, and often hypocritical society. Kuzmin emphasizes the normality of gay domestic life, even as he insists on his right to extend this domesticity to other men besides his partner. It's a difficult position, and a very difficult experience, given the prevailing hypocrisy and lies about this in our country. Such a stance turns out to be much more radical than that of someone like Yaroslav Mogutin, who "shocked" Moscow society a few years ago with his advocacy of a carnivalesque Nietzschean gay promiscuity. The profligate, the libertine, even if he's gay, is fully acceptable—he does not call society's moral foundations into question. The idea of non-traditional relationships and the simultaneous acceptance of traditional family values, especially if the person openly follows his principles in life, is much more serious, because it attacks the comfortable Russian status quo—on the one hand, "sinning shamelessly and unceasingly," and on the other a tireless sanctimony.

In a sign of protest, Kuzmin dramatizes this topic in his public life as well as in his poems: openly embracing boyfriends and walking with them arm-in-arm down the street, taking them to readings, etc. He is also an activist for gay culture, for example in his launch of the gay literary magazine *Risk*.

I track two basic experiences in Kuzmin that inform his poems. First, his romantic and sexual life. Second, his interactions with "the people." What does "the people" refer to? For Kuzmin, who is a dyed-in-the-wool intellectual, "the people" is always a different world—sometimes touching, sometimes nightmarish, but always chaotic and impenetrable. Given Kuzmin's drive toward systemization, however, "the people" is first and foremost the bearer of chaos. And any confrontation with them affects the author so much that it is, as far as one can tell, his most powerful creative stimulant and source of subject matter. The girl begging for cookies in Minsk, the boy writing funny words in his diary on the metro…

A tall boy
in a black shirt
was being pelted by the rain
(to get out of it
he hopped on this bus).

The little pimples on his sunburnt arms
make the little hairs on them
more noticeable.
If you were to run your hand
through his hair, that's been cut too short,
he'd hit you in the face.

I stand next to him in silence.

He hops off.
And through the window I see him walking,
uncomfortably slow.

Kuzmin's subject—"the people"—and his romantic themes are of course related. The boys he often writes about in his poems are the thread that binds Kuzmin to and in some ways reconciles him with "the people." They are, on the one hand, the flesh of his flesh;

and, on the other, entirely foreign, threatening, strange. However, there is an important detail: if, according to gay mythology, their depravity, vitality, and criminality usually give boys from this social stratum a special charm (recall Genet and Pasolini), then Kuzmin, I think, finds the opposite—that homosexuality is a kind of element in the culture, the cosmos, a harmonious element in the chaotic plebeian consciousness. Therefore, unquestionably, Kuzmin subconsciously associates promoting tolerance for gays with the taming of the Russian chaos. That is, he considers it a missionary's task. It's no revelation to say that Kuzmin, in his own view, is a missionary, a cultural colonizer, which goes along with...

But more on that later.

It's worth saying a little more about his technique. Kuzmin's best poems are aimed toward the most valuable and most elusive feature of "objectivist" free verse: transparency—as though there were no text at all, but instead, reality itself shining through the text. In his poems there are almost no standard features of Russian verse: no acceleration, bursts of irrational language, or charged material launching the poet into the future. Kuzmin doesn't need this kind of propulsion; his task is to capture the instant, to find the exact words for its sense, to remain in the present.

> My first lover
> is sitting across from me in the metro.
> He doesn't see me.
> Or doesn't recognize me.
> No, no, he doesn't see me—
> still.
> How many years have passed?
> In the opening of his t-shirt
> the hairs on his chest.

Sometimes Kuzmin misfires; he is too direct, or he is too demotic. At these points his very serious struggle becomes visible. What is the field of this struggle? On the one hand, it is the depiction of homosexuality as one of the many human possible overtones, one of many threads connecting people and events, and therefore something that can be isolated and regarded as a specifically *cultural* phenomenon. On the other hand, it is the depiction of homosexuality as an association, whether random or deliberate, that eventually becomes a necessary emotional attachment to a concrete minority, an identification that especially in a hostile environment can't help but come before anything else. Antiquated linguistic turns and a sometimes overt literariness weigh down Kuzmin's writing, tug it into the past and expose the "traditionalist," the bookish boy underneath; at the same time the impulse to accelerate, to move forward, pulls him away from the "objectivity" he seeks. The author does everything to balance the past and the future, and finds himself as a result on a kind of lonely border. I really like his poems. They seem harmless enough, but you can see a very serious struggle taking place inside them.

\\\

Some people think Kuzmin is a kind of snob, someone who enjoys clever verbiage for its own sake and deliberately publishes texts that the average reader cannot understand. But that's just not true. Now, Kuzmin *will* sometimes say something so very, very clever, but at the same time so unbelievably stupid—or recite some pretentious nonsense—that you want to tell him "Dima, you're an idiot," as, I recall, one woman at a reading did indeed once tell him. But overall, although he can be too smart for his own good, his emotions and his intellect complement one another. He has a healthy disdain for philosophical or poetic abstraction, and has mostly avoided the baffling and often self-parodying sophistry of modern French philosophy. He holds these things at a distance because in the end he is an educator and colonizer, and needs to speak in a language comprehensible to people. Not in a *simplified* language, but in an accessible one. The point isn't that he doesn't occasionally use words or intonations that might irritate or annoy a person with an anti-intellectual bent, because he does; the point is that what he actually produces are still comprehensible words and sentiments.

Kuzmin has many critics. They are both individual critics and representatives of other institutions. His main competitor within the poetic field is the influential, "establishment" poetry magazine *Arion*. Who are these people? Professionally, the editors are college professors (one teaches Shakespeare), with a sideline in literary criticism; ideologically, they are political liberals with a strongly conservative aesthetic bias. Underlying all their beliefs is the concept of "normal" poetry. This poetry can be good or bad, entirely talentless or full of genius: what's important is that it's created by people with a *normal* idea of what poetry is. Normal, to *Arion's* editors, corresponds approximately to the early 20th century—that is, Mandelstam, Akhmatova, Khodasevich. All further developments, beginning with the Futurists in poetry, Duchamp in the visual arts, and so on, are incomprehensible. Even when *Arion* tries to be objective and give things their due (and this is rare enough), the extent to which the situation is hopeless and will never change is clear, in fact it's clearest then. All that interests them is their sort of poetry, whether from the Soviet era or today. Almost everything else is lumped in with "the avant-garde."

We should give the *Arion* editors their due—they sense the threat embodied by Kuzmin. In fact they consider it their task continuously to expose him and his project, devoting an article to Vavilon in almost every issue of the magazine. But in the end, for all their relentless polemicizing, the editors are also profoundly complacent, convinced that time is on their side: "Everything will fall into place eventually, and the young Akhmatovas, Mandelstams, and Khodaseviches our journal promotes will assume their rightful positions in the history of poetry, having pushed aside the contemporary charlatans who make more noise."

But even if you put the question this way (which you can't— that's the fatal flaw of the *Arion* people, they still think it's 1913), then, alas, 90 percent of the contemporary "Akhmatovas,"

"Mandelstams," and "Khodaseviches" would come out of Vavilon. That is, the playing field is totally uneven, in fact the *Arion* editors don't even seem to know where the game is being held. There are no Acmeists anymore, there are no Futurists. The ignorance of the *Arion* editors, it should be said, is closely related to a total lack of understanding of the structure of modern society. *Arion* has managed to inherit the worst characteristics of the old Soviet bureaucracy—its reluctance to modernize on the one hand, and its desire to completely dominate the cultural field on the other. As a result, *Arion* has failed in recent years to find or adopt a single original position, and in the near future it will likely degrade into total worthlessness. In truth, I wouldn't have bothered to devote so much space to *Arion* if his confrontation with them hadn't taken up so much space in Dmitry's life.

Another system in competition with Kuzmin's is that of the web poets, who are typically united by one or another online institution, with its own hierarchy, authorities, and ideologues. By "web poets" I don't just mean anyone who publishes his poems online (Vavilon, after all, is itself in large part a web project), but rather a particular type—someone whose entire metier is the web, who uses it to host his poems, arguments, declarations, etc. Your average web poet is very conservative. He omits practically the entire Bronze era (except maybe Brodsky), while the later movements—conceptualism and the like—provoke outright malice. There is a Gold and a Silver era (that is, the early 19th and early 20th centuries, respectively), and, with them, Soviet poetry in its "better" manifestations. The situation resembles *Arion* a bit, though the cheerful amateur graphomania at, say, www.poems.ru is on the whole more attractive than the professional tedium produced by the tenured liberals. The one well-known writer who concentrates within his person all the ideas of the web poets, and who, as a result, apparently has the greatest authority among them, is Dmitry Bykov. Bykov is a poet who, as it were, validates the entire web poetry project with his existence, and gives it hope: so it turns out it is possible to be a post-Soviet reactionary and an excellent contemporary poet and writer! Bykov really is a striking figure, but it is precisely his uniqueness that proves this to be a dead-end. What was good for him (e.g., Soviet prose and verse) may well be poison for others.

Since web poetry is a kind concentrated portrait of the Russian unconscious, a collection of its most painful neuroses, it sometimes manifests itself as an inert, conservative, and very aggressive mass. Naturally, the characteristic philistine hatred toward Kuzmin finds full expression here. Kuzmin is accused of just about everything, including being a Jew, a fag, and also selling out for Western grants. It should be said that there exists an idea in Russia that our young poets write free verse exclusively so they can be studied by Western Slavists and invited by them to Western institutions. Meanwhile, as far as I know, Kuzmin has received exactly one grant in his entire life—for writing a pamphlet about gay life in Russia. Really, the irony is that NO ONE can boast of having created a project of this scope (in addition to everything else, Kuzmin has by this point probably overseen the publication of several hundred books) totally independently, with his own money, or, more accurately, with his lover's money, who earned it as a computer programmer and web administrator—for which many people, including myself, are profoundly grateful to him.

There does exist one very attractive position, within the poetic field, that is distinct from Kuzmin's. It is represented by people who are on the whole sympathetic to Kuzmin's project, though they happen to diverge from him on some things. This is the poetry series OGI, which has existed for a few years now and which was supported by, among others, Mikhail Aizenberg and Nikolai Okhotin. *These are very erudite people with a very strong intuitive feel for poetry.* The books chosen for OGI prove their intelligence and showcase their ideas about what mainstream contemporary poetry ought to be. This mainstream can be pretty diverse, but it has its limits—simply because the range of any individual person's sense or tastes has its limits, even if we're talking about a very erudite, very sensitive person. Whereas Kuzmin is doing something different; he is, in a sense, not expressing his personal preferences at all in his project, or only enough so that the project can exist: the total ecological approach is in part a rejection of individual taste.

To sum up: Any attempt to pit another system of thought from within the poetic field against Kuzmin's radical inclusiveness is ill-conceived. With the exception of out-and-out mass culture, every rival system is already to some extent included in the Kuzmin paradigm. No less important is the fact that every single one of Kuzmin's rivals holds to a half-hearted, compromised—in short, historically doomed—world view. Kuzmin, by contrast, offers a whole-hearted project that combines aesthetic, ideological, political, and ethical principles. Principles, their irrefutable presence—these are, as we've said, Dmitry Kuzmin's most important quality. He and I quarreled once over one of my poems. He was preparing to publish the poem on his site, but there were two things about it he didn't like: first, the word *cocksucker*; second, the use of unreliable, essentially false information about Alexander Lukashenko, the president of Belarus. We settled on a compromise: Kuzmin let me have my *cocksucker* and added an editor's footnote about Lukashenko[32]. Of course, you could argue that if you're going to accept an author, then you should give him the opportunity to say what he wants in the way that he wants to say it. But in this case, although I argued with him, I completely understood and even approved of Kuzmin, especially against the background of the complete ideological bankruptcy I saw all around me.

\\\

Principles are a powerful instrument in a world that is slowly transforming people into spineless rats. But the presence of principles creates serious problems for the person who has them. For example, the Kuzmin principle of maximal liberalism and tolerance toward different poetics, which in its social manifestation assumes

---

32   The poem in question is "Europe" (pg. 83).

individuals' and minorities' tolerance of one another, creates difficulties for Kuzmin as a political thinker, because—

> Because no liberalism can extend itself to the point of self-annihilation. The courts, the police, the United Nations, that's all well and good, but let's not put the cart before the horse: first, axiology. Then ethics. And then justice. Not the other way around. I happen to have a lot of experience in this respect, particularly in the realm of throwing drunk jerks out of public spaces, be it from a subway car or a literary reading—because, unfortunately, there is no alternative. And because there aren't enough police officers for every metro car, and because often the same scum are working for the police (and are often just as drunk). What do you propose? Asking the UN, where Libya and North Korea have the same right to vote as everyone else, for permission to depose Saddam Hussein? It's a jury trial in which half the jury arrived in court straight from a maximum security prison. And, yes, probably even such a jury could be handled: you promise to lower one criminal's sentence, wave a bunch of cash in front of another, and in the end Libya votes for the use of force in Iraq. From a political point of view, that's probably the ideal outcome. But I am not a politician, and I am not obliged to judge from a political point of view. Ethics and axiology concern me. I am convinced that social order does not originate with the irreproachable work of the courts and the police, but rather with a civilian's sense of justice. And this sense of justice relies on nothing but one's moral principles.

This is Kuzmin in 2003, arguing with the writer Oleg Dark about the invasion of Iraq. On the one hand, what we have here is the declaration of an anarchist. On the other, Kuzmin has always had an enormous will to power—power here in the sense of supplying order on many different levels, from the most abstract to the most everyday. There are stories about him going from room to room in the Moscow State dormitory throwing drunk people out. And there are probably witnesses to the times when Kuzmin personally dealt with "drunk jerks" at literary events. I witnessed an incident of this kind just once. It involved the fairly well-known poet Eremenko[33]. On the evening in question he arrived at a festival of youth poetry in the capacity of a drunk jerk. I watched him. He was excited, he kept shifting around—clearly something was going on in the respected poet's head. For example, when Kuzmin began to say that the poet Anashevich hadn't yet shown up, Eremenko shouted something along the lines of "Anashevich'll be here soon! He's just catching a cab!" At one point between readings, Eremenko approached the stage and yelled, "Your country's at war!!" in the sense of, "And you're doing fuck-knows-what here in the meantime."

After this had been going on for some time, Kuzmin finally said from the stage: "Security, remove this hooligan from the room." No one reacted, and Kuzmin repeated his command several times. Eremenko was taken out. Afterward, a few of the readers refused to go on stage in protest. Later, Kuzmin would call Eremenko a has-been, a "former poet," and so on. Was there something else behind this conflict? I don't know. I remember Kuzmin saying somewhere that in the late Soviet period there used to be an annual contest called "King of the Poets," and he made the finals two years in a row. The first time, Eremenko was his opponent, and the jury said: "Well, Dmitry is still a young poet; we'll hear more from him, no doubt," and gave the prize to Eremenko. Then the next year, Kuzmin made the finals alongside, apparently, some unknown poet, and the jury said, "Well, Dmitry Kuzmin, that's someone we've all heard of already," and gave the prize to the unknown. Did that old slight play a role here? I don't know. On the evening of the Eremenko incident, I was basically on Kuzmin's side, although it was an ambiguous situation. It would have been significantly less ambiguous had Kuzmin simply thrown Eremenko out himself, as he'd thrown others out. And in my opinion, there is a fundamental, I mean a truly archetypal difference, between doing it yourself, and calling for the guards.

---

33   Alexander Eremenko (1950–). "Metarealist" poet.

\\\

At what point did I begin to lose interest—not so much in Kuzmin personally as in Vavilon as a whole, and the literary world in general? I had sensed differences between myself and the majority of Vavilonians from the start, but I never took them seriously. The turning point probably came with the Iraq War. After the American invasion, Kuzmin organized an event called "We Love America." Like much in his life, this was a response: some time before, a small group of writers in Moscow had held a protest against the United States. It should be said that such a protest was perfectly natural, seeing as at the time MILLIONS of people across Europe were taking to the streets to protest the war. But Kuzmin and his friends still had nightmares about the Russian people's "deep-seated anti-Americanism" (and its accompanying anti-Westernism, anti-liberalism, anti-Semitism), and these fears wiped out any considerations they would otherwise have had as intellectuals, or even just as sensate beings.

I was already familiar with Kuzmin's thoughts on American foreign policy. "Crush without mercy," he said to me after September 11, meaning crush the terrorists. And in his correspondence with Oleg Dark from 2003, he was perfectly explicit. He believes it was a mistake to grant independence to Third World countries in the 20th century, that it led to massive fatalities, and he therefore has nothing in particular against colonialism, or the use of force to maintain order in "backward" countries.

That was one of my reasons for splitting with Kuzmin. Of course, political views should not be the reason for splitting with someone. Actually, no. It is *precisely* political views that should be the reason, because politics is not soccer; your affiliation is not something you wear on Saturdays and then put away for the rest of the week. And there is a sense in which some of the things we value about soccer, or culture more generally—consensus, coexistence, "peace"—are impossible in politics, not because only one side can win, but because, as a result of its winning, everything will change.

Because real politics is participation, it's involvement and transformation, and if individual poetics can only coexist in the form of texts, in an anthology, a.k.a. in a dead form, in "eternity," then in life they inevitably come into conflict.

The social order known as postmodernism or late capitalism, which came into full flower in Russia in the 1990s, was geared in many ways toward the prevention of such conflict and thus the conservation of a certain status quo. What was this status quo? For a long time, I followed readers' reactions to my and my colleagues' poetry with great interest. If those reactions could speak in a common voice, they would say approximately this: "We like you, we enjoy you, you're unusual, talented, we value and respect you. But you will never have anything to do with our lives. You won't push us one centimeter from the path we're on, even if we ourselves don't know what that path is or where it's going. We will read your texts and go back to doing what we were doing before. Thank you." That is, a person sincerely, intelligently, and emotionally experiences a text. But this text exerts no influence on him whatsoever. This is, of course, an unconscious attitude, but it is total and it is produced by the common *condition*. And, of course, for the artist it raises the question—how else would I have wanted it? To have my poetry be celebrated by "the people"? To be carried through the streets on their shoulders? Well, no. I don't know. Let's put that question aside for the moment.

The main strategy developed in the poetic field to break down the comfortable tolerance of postmodern society is the so-called "straightforward utterance." This is a movement that tries firmly to establish the connection between the author and the text, often by calling attention to the author and resurrecting him after his murder by the postmodernists; it thereby tries to escape the limits of that text and lay claim to a truth outside of it. Kuzmin has called this movement "post-conceptualist"—that is, it senses acutely the postmodern death of the author and the necessity for his resurrection and rehabilitation.

Post-conceptualism comes after the radical word-play and author-assassination of writers like Dmitri Prigov and Vladimir Sorokin (in his early work)—that is, after the Russian representatives of early postmodernism had become canonical. It can come in several forms, which in my view can be usefully divided into the ultra-conservative, the theatrical, and the leftist. The ultra-conservative tendency rejects the entire rhetoric of contemporary humanism—its *texts, discourses, civil societies, human rights*, as well as its *engaged art* and *innovative poetics*—in favor of a poetics that claims a different ontological basis, whether it is God or Mother Russia or (often) both. The theatrical tendency subsumes all meaning beneath that of performance, presence, and event—that is, beneath the immediate experience of the text. All else is vanity and (especially) tedium. The final, leftist version of straightforward utterance attacks the liberal concept of the private individual (and reader), whose existence masks the true nature of bourgeois society. For a leftist art, there are no individuals: there is simply a single human space in which people exist. And between these people are the most varied connections, be they hidden or obvious. Bourgeois politics and culture attempt not to rectify this situation, but to regulate and preserve it by different means—in our era, under the guise of morality, equal rights, multiculturalism, and "free and diverse expression." But no work of art is a thing in itself, as bourgeois thought claims, nor is it a divine reflection, as religious thought claims, but evidence of all of society's defects, including the relations of the dominant and dominated. The task of innovative art is to insist on the uniqueness of the individual while revealing the genuine relations between people, the true connections in society, and, as a result, to forge a new reality.

And what does Kuzmin say to all this? Approximately the following: *This is all well and good, but I'm a simple man. I care about the text. And I know that works created from rigidly defined ideological positions are often of very low quality. Of course, I am more than happy to publish any exceptions to that rule. In other words, while my existence may be an obstacle to your truth, your existence is in no way an obstacle to mine. I can tolerate any one of you. As long as it's of a high enough quality, and not overtly fascistic or Stalinoid (that is, anti-human), then I'm happy to include your work in my poetic system.*

The three positions above are whole and indivisible, in contrast to those half-formed and compromised types of consciousness I described earlier when talking about Kuzmin's rivals. In contemporary young Russian poetry, the three positions can be identified with Dmitry Sokolov[34], Dmitry Vodennikov[35], and me. Our development from our earliest experiments, which Kuzmin approved, published, and promoted, to where we are today, ideologically and aesthetically, shows the arcs that these three paths are likely to take. And it's notable that the artistic and ideological positions of all three of us today are now alien to Kuzmin.

\\\

Not long after deciding to leave the literary world, I happened to run into Kuzmin. I told him what I planned to do. "Well, then, a new era is coming," he said thoughtfully. And on that note we parted. For some time he didn't seem to understand what was happening, and whether he ought to interpret my gesture as hostile. Eventually he settled on hostile. From then on he would occasionally write that Medvedev had lost his mind, what a sad fate, he has been forgotten, etc. Of course, a person who's fallen out of Kuzmin's network must inevitably fade away and be lost

---

34   Dmitry Sokolov (1975–). In the 1990s, Sokolov's poetry was aligned with Vavilon; his first book, published by Argo-Risk, received some acclaim. Afterward, he left poetry behind to work as a journalist under the name Dmitry Sokolov-Mitrich. In 2007, he published a book about how Chechens and Tajiks victimize the Russian populace.

35   Dmitry Vodennikov (1968–). A confessional poet, considered the forerunner of the New Sincerity, and one of the most popular poets in Russia today. He wrote the introduction to Medvedev's first book. Also works in theater and collaborates with hip bands.

forever—that's a given. And no doubt there have been poets who broke with Kuzmin and then stopped writing, started drinking, became "former poets," and so on, just as he says. But it doesn't hurt to gently help that process along, remind the public from time to time that there once was this guy, and then he lost his mind, and everyone forgot him. He's not the first, nor will he be the last. As Vodennikov, another very interesting and very important person to me, once wrote: *I know you want it this one way—but it's not going to happen.* I was naturally very upset to read these revelations on Kuzmin's blog. Not for myself, so much, but for Kuzmin, because, for example, "Medvedev has lost his mind," written about a person whose behavior you obviously do not understand but suspect may be a threat to you, echoes again not so much the traditions of the underground as those of the Tsarist censor Pavel Famusov, and the Soviet Union of Writers, and the KGB.

It turned out that in addition to everything else my "escape" became a kind of test, of Dmitry Kuzmin personally, but also of the limits of his project. Here was a man who considered himself my primary, my sole, benefactor, and what would he think of me—alive but no longer connected to his project, even, in a sense, criticizing it? Kuzmin's desire to direct, structure, and name the currents of contemporary poetry helped many poets who without him would never have been noticed or brought to light. But any ambitious, large-scale project reaches a point when it enters into conflict with the private ambitions of its creator—it's a sign that the project has *outgrown* him—and for it to advance, for the project to develop, the creator has to humble himself, has to ease up a little. At the point when Kuzmin should have restrained his ambitions and his grudge, he lacked the strength, and he lost, because only a project that adopts the most radical forms of self-critique can keep going.

But what did I want? A pat on the head? No, not exactly. I wanted Kuzmin to admit (if not publicly, then at least to himself) that even after leaving Vavilon I remained an ally, because we were fighting the same fight—pursuing new possibilities for existence in poetry and in life. Only now, I would need to be judged according to my criteria, not his, and, what's more, if he valued me for myself, and not merely as a part of his project, then he would try to understand those new criteria. And yet, *no liberalism can extend itself to the point of self-annihilation.*

\\\

A little more about postmodernism and the will to power, and the ways in which the conflict between me and Kuzmin, which at some level is merely personal, did, I think, reveal important things about our respective projects. In the wake of my "escape," some of my poems, for various reasons (including, presumably, just plain inertia), continued to appear in various places, and Kuzmin would occasionally comment to the effect of, essentially, *Medvedev says he won't publish anymore, but he continues to publish anyway. And that's all right,* Kuzmin would say, quoting Foucault, *because "the author is but a means of organizing texts."* By which he meant: *Medvedev may have written the texts, but what we publishers do with them is not his concern, and anyway the sense in which he can be said to have written them is very limited indeed.*

I found it really sad to see the words of a writer like Foucault, who spent his whole life battling against and exposing power in its various forms, used as a pure, absolute, and rather crude instrument of power. It highlighted, for me, the gap between the time when the ideas of the postmodern fathers held a revolutionary charge, and our time, when you can use them precisely as Kuzmin does. Foucault meant, approximately, that the text speaks in ways that the author sometimes did not intend; that a text, in order to exist, must pass through an author, who structures and arranges it, but this does not mean he can completely control a text or answer for all of its meanings. In the battle against logo- and phallo-centrism, this was, unquestionably, a progressive idea. But when Kuzmin uses it in response to my questions about liberal concepts of intellectual property (and their violation), he is either being obtuse or unscrupulous, or a bit of both. In any case, it proves once again that Kuzmin's thought was and remains hemmed in by the postmodernist framework, proves that he, despite himself being a fully living author, doesn't need any kind of "rebirth of the author" at all. Because a living author is a constant unpredictability and inconvenience, a constant threat to a structured space, and even to his own texts within that space. A living and developing author inevitably changes and recodes his past work, which may likewise compel his public to reevaluate it.

In short: Kuzmin's system, not in itself but in the general literary context, reproduces the structure of a repressively tolerant society. Yes, Vavilon accepts all "innovative" poetics, but the general course is set by people with a specific socio-professional status, with specific values and a specific worldview, who, accordingly, are expressing their specific group or class interests. It makes perfect sense that perhaps the central literary tendency in Vavilon was the so-called "new sincerity": the appeal to personal experience (child-hood; romantic and sexual encounters; family life) to the exclusion of social and political experience, justifying this by appealing to its authenticity (personal, emotional, etc.)[36]. It makes sense that it was amid the class of designers, copy-writers, and glossy magazine journalists—in a word, traders in appearances (I, too, belong to this class to a certain extent, although I really wish I didn't belong to it)—that this "new sincerity" developed. A direct and very personable form of writing, it helped authors continue in their lucrative professional lives by offering them the possibility of genuine creativity in the place of the "creativity" they're supposed to produce at the office, all the while leaving the gap between the lyric hero and the social status of the author intact. The gap is left intact because crossing it could lead to unpleasant self-interrogation, and doubt, and even a rejection of the social order that allows all this to go on.

---

36   For more on the New Sincerity movement, see the essay "Literature Will Be Tested" (pg. 231).

This is not some grand conspiracy on Kuzmin's part, but the result of perfectly objective processes—the most progressive and creative people find themselves in demand for the leading creative positions while simultaneously creating the most progressive art. But that does not mean we should acquiesce to this state of affairs—it ought to be resisted. Because it seems to me that no matter how the world looked in 1989 or 1991—and I know it looked different from how it looks today—we can all now admit that the notion of post-industrial capitalism as the best of all possible worlds is hardly the most progressive notion available.

\\\

All of which merely demonstrates, once again, that the way to overcome the postmodern is to reevaluate the relationship between author and work, text and reality, politics and art.

Kuzmin writes:

> There's a war going on here on Earth, and there have been victims on both sides—but one of those sides is mine.

I think these are monstrous words. Rereading them, I see that everything that happened between us was not an accident. Why? The entire progressive intellectual tradition of the 20th century has tried to oppose large-scale government-engineered projects and geopolitical divisions. And yet today's intellectual—who values these traditions—will sometimes conveniently forget that, for example, his ability to realize his wonderful particularity, uniqueness, and inimitability (in his creative endeavors and rich and varied personal life) is available to him and other Europeans thanks to the fact that his government buys natural gas at a reduced price from the tyrant of Turkmenistan. The tyrant is happy to keep prices low because, being a tyrant, he can keep some of the profits for himself while closing village libraries and hospitals. Should the tyrant cut off the natural gas—if, for example, he is deposed by an angry mob of his countrymen—then our hypothetical European intellectual will have less time, strength, and money for being creative, and pursuing his fascinating personal life, and developing his inimitable, beautiful, God-given individuality. The same is true of our European's oil, and coal, and so on. And, well, what of it? Should we stop writing poems? Go crazy from guilt? No. No. We just need to transform our picture of the world a little, and we can begin by ceasing to talk nonsense about the clash of civilizations.

Because otherwise you become an appendage of the system that allows you to take up whatever art you want, develop whatever styles, discourses, and poetics you want, on the condition that you do not interfere with politics, with real life. And your "grown-up" credo (and, clearly, a reasonable and obedient member of the contemporary neoliberal system is first and foremost a GROWN-UP, as opposed to all those idealists, pseudo-rebels, and dreamers, who aren't) will go like this: *I am a humble man, my business is putting together words.* As for everyone else, I think they should do what they want. And my ability to think this way is based in part on a gigantic military, and low electricity prices, and plenty of oil.

And this does not strike me as an idea befitting the glory of liberalism, which was once a progressive and salvational force in human history; and it does not strike me as an argument for individuation. This is society as armed camp, as colonizer, as exploiter. It is an indication that liberal concepts have entered a period of exhaustion, when their proponents often find themselves trampling their own norms in the most cynical and vicious ways possible.

Because there are no private people, and there are no two (or three, or four) clashing civilizations. There is a united space in which people exist. And between those people, as between poetics, are the most varied connections, be they hidden or obvious. Disentangling these connections, overcoming old connections and creating new ones, the spontaneous invention and formation of radically new groups—work that casts doubt on the prevailing national, religious, civilizational, sexual, and—yes—economic differences—*that* is the path to solidarity, that is the path to a new world. It is impossible to restrain, cancel out, or quash the passion, obstinacy, vanity, and pride of the Zapatistas, the idealist poets, and Islamic extremists, because one cannot quash or cancel out the voices of the cultures that stand behind them—all one can do is redirect or transform, but only on the individual level and only *as oneself*; and to do this, one must put one's private life, and vanity, and the messianism characteristic of minorities (gays, Jews, and the intelligentsia in general) into the service of this new task. This is the course of progressive culture in its relation to the new politics, which should replace the corpse of politics that is decaying right now across the whole world, but especially in Russia. Only *that* will be the movement forward. Maybe it won't be successful, maybe it will fail, but it will be A GENUINE DEVELOPMENT OF THE GLOBAL HUMANISTIC TRADITION.

I wouldn't want to end on such a pathetic note. Beyond the question of whether I am right or wrong, Kuzmin remains an extremely important and symptomatic figure, possessing within himself a grand duality—his colossal service, his progressive, even revolutionary and distinct position within the Russian culture of the last twenty years, and his rather unattractive, reactionary position in the context of global culture as a whole. I think his project, as of now, is a complete success; its future fate, however, whether it will stagnate (in the conceptual sense) and become entirely conventional, legitimizing the pseudo-tolerance of neoliberal authority (and it is specifically in such a role that Kuzmin's project could be useful to the authorities, or desirable), or progress and become an alternative source, offering a real democratic and potentially traumatic diversity (that is constantly calling its own coordinates into question), depends on Kuzmin's future conduct, and the future of Russian and global politics.

ON LITERATURE
[poems]

Selections from the cycle "For Eternity"
(published at kirillmedvedev.narod.ru, April 2005)
and from *3%: Poems from 2005-2006* (Free Marxist Press, 2007).

Translations by Keith Gessen

\\\

Everyone knows that the Lit. Institute trains writers,
but everyone also knows that the only ones who become writers
are those who got thrown out
of the Lit. Institute.

Or, at the very least, were outsiders there.

But there is
one particular writer there,
a kind of anti-hero,
a small man of middling talent
but insatiable will to power.

He is dictatorial when he needs to be,
and groveling when that is more appropriate.

He is, when necessary, a patriot
(and how many little insects are dining out
these days
on their newfound patriotism!).

I left the Lit. Institute a long time ago
but I keep up with the gossip.

This particular person never did me any harm,
one time during an oral exam he said
something to the effect of:
"How is it that you write for the magazine
International Literature
but say such ridiculous things during this exam?"

And he was right!!

Not long ago it became clear
that this man was about to become the president
of the Lit. Institute, and finally the faculty and students
got together and made sure
this didn't happen.

The publishing house of the Lit. Institute put out his book of
    stories,
but that wasn't the thing—
the thing isn't what he tells about himself
but what he is.
Sergei Petrovich Tolkachev,
a short man, forty years old,
a fully formed, if, of course, second-rate literary type,
sitting at a college, preparing second-rate writers,

I sometimes recall the Lit. Institute, this separate world,
it's no worse and no better than other worlds,
and those who run the place,
and those unhappy ones who leave it only when they're dead,
and those honest and brilliant ones, who get kicked out,
and those honest and weak ones,
who stay—

I see them all together in one place
as if on a separate creased page
of my life.

\\\

I'm standing here turning the pages
of a book by a young Petersburg poet,
with a funny kind of aggravation,
and sympathy,
with some slight irony.
I watch the things
this city makes,
no one is as close to the source of poetry,
to the world's ice,
attached to it through some special,
if seriously polluted,
pipeline.
I didn't think I could still take pleasure
in the cold harmony
of the world,
from the only possible right combination of words—
standing here, turning over these sweet conservative *verses*,
which you need to read
over tea, with milk,
in a bathrobe (!) (?),
and imagine yourself
in a hungry city,
a cold city during the war,
with the books of your favorite poets,
wondering which of them to throw
in the stove for heat,
and which to exchange
for some bad herring and a loaf of bread.

and then to *find* yourself in a hungry
city, in a cold building,
and imagine yourself sitting
with tea, and milk,

in a bathrobe,
turning the pages of your favorite book,
and taking pleasure
from the cold hopeless harmony,
from the gentle melodious word-picture,
from the only possible right combination of words.

in short, everything's all right with this book,
and "Denis Sheremetyev,"
is, of course, the only possible right name
for its author[37].

so everything's all right, but—
but what?

no, no, no, everything's all right.

but still, maybe,
something's missing?
no, nothing's missing.

maybe the problem is that
I'm turning the pages of this book
in a store that got blown up a few days ago
and still smells like dried fish,
and everywhere, on the tables, on the shelves,
you can see the edges of burned books?

no, that's not it.

art, as we know, is higher
than all that.

---

37   The book is probably *Ulika* ("Clue"), Pushkinsky Fond, 2004. The name
Sheremetyev suggests a Russian aristocratic lineage.

actually, I don't believe that,
but for now, so that this poem
works out,
I believe it.

and this book's a little burnt too, actually,
but it's okay, see, it survived.

so everything's all right.
although, maybe the fact that
everything's all right is the problem?
no, that's not a problem.

or maybe it's that when everything's all right,
that just doesn't sit well with me?
no, it sits well.
…
(then what the hell?)

\\\

I've seen crumbling ridges,
and sea ports, and terrible towns.
but an asshole like you
that's something new.

a man who hires a prostitute
gives her more than he pays,
and she gives him more
than he pays her.

then where does the surplus go,
why are they both cheated?

it doesn't go anywhere, actually, it just disappears,
it melts into their mutual kindness,
it burns
in their feast of kindness and self-sacrifice,
and that's why in the morning there's frustration—
hysterics, anger—
she wants someone who won't
pay anymore,
and he wants someone who would
only take—
and each of them needs some pressure—
egoism or cruelty,
their own or someone else's, it doesn't matter,
but so that one of them would get it,
so that one of them would be satisfied.
this is called: "I need love"
the kind that causes pain,
that causes music
music plays
and the one who's going to sell her tomorrow,

that is, in essence, the pimp, the seller,
he knows her better than anyone, and loves her selflessly.
a pretty girl hands out cigarettes near the metro,
but smiles at me for free—
and there's nothing anyone can do about it.
and only me, I'm the only one who thinks
everything's bought and paid for,
I'm the only sad asshole who thinks that,
even if not everything's bought and paid for yet,
not everything's stamped out,
even if you can still win some kind of prize,
it's still going to turn out
to be a boot full of someone else's bad wine.

— — —

oh, I know why I have so many bones to pick with you
my friends:
you're naive, and so pure,
you're blameless;
and I wanted to take your sins upon my head
(if only you'd had some).

Medvedev's first public action took place in January 2005, when he protested "Russia2," an "alternative" art exhibit at the Central House of Artists in Moscow. "What alternative can these people, products of the corrupt 1990s, present to the current bourgeois-fascistoid mainstream?" Medvedev asked in a leaflet that he handed out in front of the exhibit. The concept of a separate artistic space in Putin's Russia, he argued, "is conformist and hypocritical, because anyone can see that there can be no 'parallel' space—if the authorities decide to pressure art again, then everyone will fall in line—the salon will return to the salon, and the underground to the underground." Medvedev called his action "SchizOpposition: A Farewell to Moscow Actionism"—the fact that this was the title of his action, Medvedev noted in the account of it published on his website, "was indicated by the writing on my clothing."

In the next two years, Medvedev performed other public actions, including organizing a rock concert in Moscow in support of striking workers and rolling a pear through the streets of the city during Victory Day (May 9). In 2006, he joined the socialist movement Vpered (Forward). In October 2006, he started a LiveJournal blog at zoltan-partosh.livejournal.com. (Zoltan Partosh was Medvedev's great-grandfather. A Hungarian poet, translator, pediatrician, and communist, he fled to the Soviet Union with his family in 1919 after the revolution in Hungary was put down. Partosh was briefly arrested during the purges of the 1930s— Georg Lukács wrote a letter vouching for him—but then released. He died in Moscow in 1959.)

Posted at zoltan-partosh.livejournal.com
October 23, 2006

Translation by Keith Gessen

Why I Started a LiveJournal Blog
(for those who are interested)

My sense is that a certain period of time has come to an end.

For me this was the period of spontaneous civic poetry, which never took place. What comes now is the period of stern and sober political choices; cruel analysis; and serious action. Though these, too, probably won't happen.

But there will still be lots of extra emotions and many extra words. Mine, too. And everything that I've needed to say IMMEDIATELY in the past five years by way of poetry (or at least in my understanding of poetry), I've said. And most of what I've tried to understand while moving away from the literary world, I've understood. Therefore I've made the choice not to publish any more poems anywhere for the next five years. If I write them, I will write them knowing that no one will read them for at least five years. And if that means I don't write anything, then that means I don't need to write anything.

I will continue to sing songs and write some things, here among other places.

HOW'S THIS FOR A POEM?

[action]

In the summer of 2006, Medvedev and Vpered supported oil
and gas workers in their conflict with their employer, the giant
oil company Surgutneftegaz. The workers in Surgut were led by
a 45-year-old crane operator named Alexander Zakharin, who
organized several surprisingly large demonstrations of workers
demanding pay raises. In the fall, Surgutneftegaz fired Zakharin.
After reading an interview Zakharin gave to the press, Medvedev
arranged it into the following text.

Posted at zoltan-partosh.livejournal.com
October 31, 2006

Translation by Keith Gessen

... they decided to fire me after hours
suggesting I come by human resources at the end of the day

... they locked the door behind me
and started reading their verdict...
I had to kick at the door with my feet
so as to get my freedom...

but the crime—forceful isolation for 16 minutes—
had already taken place...

... I didn't give back my documents from the crane
(I'll give them back when they give me back my property—my
  keys, the spare parts
I installed on the crane, which I bought myself
with my own money.)

... I started trying to live on the 3,182 rubles[38] that I received for
  September,
which meant I had to go hungry...

... citing the Universal Declaration of Human Rights,
I accused the directors of Sutt-2 of discrimination...
I was paid a salary that was not sufficient to maintain
my dignity (that's in article 22,
an existence without food cannot be considered dignified)

... the Universal Declaration
of Human Rights has more legal force
than the laws of Surgutneftegaz...

... my appeals to the Presidential Representative for Human Rights
  have been fruitless...

---

38   3,182 Russian rubles converted to approximately $100 US in 2006.

… The workers will have to defend themselves

… My appeal to the President himself—
the defender of the Constitution—were also fruitless. He didn't
   defend it.

BUT IT'S ALRIGHT life goes on
and as for me, given all the free time
Surgutneftegaz has accidentally presented me with,
I INTEND TO USE IT EVERY SINGLE DAY
TO FIGHT FOR PEOPLE'S RIGHTS—THEIR HUMAN
   RIGHTS.

"Crane Operator Alexander Zakharin
Has Been Fired by Surgutneftegaz"

BRECHT IS NOT YOUR AUNT

[action]

In early 2007, Medvedev once again took to the streets. This time it was to protest the staging of a Brecht play by the well-known actor and director Alexander Kalyagin, a powerful (and popular) cultural operator who in 2005 had signed a disgraceful Soviet-style letter from fifty "representatives of culture and society" in favor of the guilty verdict against Yukos chairman Mikhail Khodorkovsky. The title of the action is a reference to Kalyagin's most famous role—as a con man who dresses up as a woman in order to impersonate someone's rich aunt in the 1975 film, *Hello, I'm Your Aunt.* What follows is Medvedev's description of the action.

Posted at Vpered.org.ru
January 25, 2007

Translation by Keith Gessen

One-Man Protest Under the Slogan,
"Mr. Kalyagin, Brecht Is Not Your Aunt!"

On January 24, a one-man protest from the socialist movement Vpered, in the person of myself, took place in front of the Et Cetera Theater in Moscow. The protest was staged in connection with the premiere of Bertolt Brecht's play, "Drums in the Night." Not long after the start of my protest, a security guard from the theater approached me and asked what I was doing there and by whose permission I was doing it.

I explained that I had every right to hold a one-man protest there without any permission from anyone.

Seeing that I would not be moved by his legal arguments, the guard took out his phone and requested "backup," but then apparently decided to resolve the problem himself. He said: "Get the fuck out of here if you don't want your face beat in." It should be noted that this man (Sergei, as it later turned out) was not your typical bemuscled security guard. He had what is known in Russia as "an intelligent face," wore glasses, and really looked more like a student from the Financial Academy or the Legal Faculty at Moscow State. Imagine my surprise, then, when after my reply to his threat that he knew where he could go, Sergei punched me in the jaw.

We were separated by some journalists and employees from the theater who ran over to us. I continued my protest. Soon after, a female administrator emerged from the theater and began talking to the journalists. She wanted to know who had commissioned the protest, how much I was being paid for it, and then began asking the journalists not to report on it. Simultaneously she was trying to calm down a very wound-up Sergei, who kept trying to involve himself in her conversation with the journalists with such remarks as: "What's he messing with our business for? Does he want his face beat in?"

At the end of the protest the administrator came over and apologized for the overeager Sergei. I suggested that the Et Cetera Theater should be more careful about the people it hires. But it should also be said that if our city's bourgeoisie continues to think that all of world culture, including leftist culture, is at its disposal to do with as it pleases, then these kinds of incidents, and problems for their "business," will be inevitable.

During the protest, leaflets with the following text were distributed:

A PROLETARIAN PLAYWRIGHT IN A COURTIER'S BOURGEOIS THEATER

The staging of a play by Bertolt Brecht, a major figure for leftist culture and the leftist movement in general, by the Et Cetera Theater is just another sign of the depoliticization of our cultural sphere, another step on the path toward the profanation and elimination of any cultural alternative, analogous to today's attempts by the authorities to destroy any political alternative, including a left and trade union movement, by pushing forward a total market fundamentalism behind the curtain of patriotic rhetoric and the so-called "national project."

The head of the Et Cetera Theater, Alexander Kalyagin, is the typical subject of this politics. He is a director-bureaucrat who, on the one hand, fights against Finance Minister German Gref's "theater reforms," but on the other hand, gives up the House of Veterans Theater in Petersburg for "commercial redevelopment." He's a member of the fictional People's Chamber; a man who welcomes the President and his suite to the theater; a signer of letters against the President's personal enemies; and the head of the Union of Theatrical Workers that fully follows the corrupt and antidemocratic line of the ruling classes.

The multifaceted activities of this theatrical boss confirm, once again, the interconnections between cultural production and the distribution of economic and political power.

For an artist to take part in this system is to support and encourage it, even as he justifies himself with the idea that "pure art is outside ideology and politics." Brecht spent his entire life battling just such ideas:

> Great apparati like the opera, the stage, the press, etc., impose their views as it were incognito. For a long time now they have taken the handiwork (music, writing, criticism, etc.) of intellectuals who share in their profits—that is, of men who are economically committed to the prevailing system but are socially near-proletarian—and processed it to make fodder for their public entertainment machine, judging it by their own standards and guiding it into their own channels; meanwhile the intellectuals themselves have gone on supposing that the whole business is concerned only with the presentation of their work, is a secondary process which has no influence over their work but merely wins influence for it. By imagining that they have got hold of an apparatus which in fact has got hold of them they are supporting an apparatus which is out of their control, which is no longer (as they believe) a means of furthering output but has become an obstacle to output, and specifically to their own output as soon as it follows a new and original course which the apparatus finds awkward or opposed to its own aims. Their output then becomes a matter of delivering the goods. And this leads to a general habit of judging works of art by their suitability for the apparatus without ever judging the apparatus by its suitability for the work.
> —from Brecht's "Notes to the Opera
> *Aufstieg und Fall der Stadt Mahogonny.*"[39]

---

39   English translation from *Brecht on Theatre: The Development of an Aesthetic*, ed. and trans. John Willett (New York, 1964), pp. 32–33.

OSTANKINO PROTEST [action]

Medvedev undertook the next action in front of the giant
Ostankino television tower in February 2007 in response to a
media scandal. Andrei Malakhov, a talk show host on Channel
One, had invited an old rocker, Vsevolod Gakkel, the cello player
from the legendary 1970s rock band Akvarium, onto his show for
a rare interview. When he came on the set, Gakkel was surprised
to find Akvarium's lead singer's ex-wife, with whom the cellist had
had an affair. Gakkel walked off the set and then wrote Malakhov,
the host, an angry open letter. The Russian blogosphere was abuzz;
Medvedev announced on his LiveJournal page that he would be
holding a protest at Ostankino.

Posted at zoltan-partosh.livejournal.com
February 28, 2007

Translation by Keith Gessen

The action announced here and in the comments sections of several other LiveJournals happened as follows:

The perimeter of the Ostankino television tower is surrounded by a metal fence with a gate; I went in the gate and approached the entrance to the tower and sat down on a bench just outside it and raised my sign: "Malakhov get out! Television for the masses, not the asses!" Shortly thereafter I was joined by Anton Ochirov (kava_bata.livejournal.com), who turned out to be the only LiveJournal user who decided to participate in the action. (I announced the action only here, on livejournal, and purposefully did not invite any friends or activists. I'd never met Anton before.) At my suggestion we sat as if separately, about three meters apart.

A cop came over and told us to get outside the fence. Anton agreed to go, which was the right thing to do insofar as he was then left alone to show his sign to the employees leaving Ostankino. I continued to sit on the bench. The cops saw that I wouldn't go quietly and called their superiors. Their superiors took about ten minutes to arrive. In the meantime the cops stood next to me and worried—there was something odd going on and they didn't have the authority to put an end to it. Then the other group of officers arrived. The senior officer took our documents. I once again refused to take down my sign, saying that I had every right to hold a one-man protest here and asking them WHERE it was written that I didn't. They told me to go across the (very wide) road, so not just outside the fence now but a good ways away. (Why not even further?) Then they started grabbing for the sign, we had a brief struggle, finally they got my sign and tore it up. This was all accompanied by strong language from both sides. Anton's sign was also taken away. Heading back into the building, the cops advised me to beat it and not ruin their night (and my own). I said something to the last of them and he stopped and we had a heated but basically good-natured exchange for the next five minutes. I told him he needs to defend the law, not break it, and he said, Let's go our separate ways and not cause each other any more problems. In other words he was basically trying to talk to me person to person, on a human level, and I kept insisting on the law, the law! We never did agree on anything, and he went back inside the tower. We left. The whole action took about 25 minutes. Thank you to Anton for participating; it was a good way to meet.

The trouble here isn't with Malakhov, of course; what I wanted to learn was what percentage of the thousand people living in Moscow and passionately discussing the Gakkel scandal on the internet would come out for an action like this—not an incredibly effective action, to be sure, but still a good deal more dignified than their fiery online whining or the banal idiocy of proclaiming that Gakkel had it coming, he should have known what he was signing up for, etc. Gakkel had it coming, of course, as do many others, but that doesn't for one second justify anyone's political uselessness, civic impotence, demagoguery, cowardice, and just plain prostitution. Which was the whole point of the exercise, of course, though I would have been happy to have been proved wrong—to have learned that a real emotional outcry (which in this case was not confined to this or that small group but seemed a genuine rejection of obvious shittiness) could become, even for just five minutes, the basis for some political action.

LITERATURE WILL BE TESTED

[essay]

Published at kirillmedvedev.narod.ru
March 2007

Translation by Mark Krotov

Literature Will Be Tested:
The Individual Project and the "New Emotionalism"

> *In old Soviet times, Brecht's claim that "a nonpartisan position,
> for art, means belonging to the ruling party," seemed to me
> the height of absurdity. Today the phrase sounds different. It
> sounds normal. Or, at least, it's something to think about.*
>
> —Lev Rubinstein

The crisis of the liberal intelligentsia's awareness of itself as a class
is the central feature of Russia's current cultural situation. For more
than fifty years the intelligentsia was defined by two things: on the
one hand, its well-known anti-statism, the view (inherited from
the revolutionary intelligentsia) of government as an overbearing,
repressive force; and, on the other hand, a cult of intimate, private
values and an antagonism (inherited from the statist, anti-revolu-
tionary authors of the *Vekhi* anthology) toward anything "leftist."
In the case of the Vekhists themselves, the antagonism was often
exacerbated by a youthful dalliance with Marxism, while in the
case of the Soviet and post-Soviet intelligentsia, it has been a matter
of ancestry: these were people descended from the revolutionaries
of 1917. Given the perfectly understandable revulsion from actually
existing Soviet socialism, the private, Vekhist attitude became the
dominant one, in particular when this intelligentsia—composed
partly of dissidents, partly of moderate non-conformists, partly of
hidden or latent anti-Soviets—achieved cultural hegemony in the
1990s atop the great wave of anti-totalitarianism. It was this liberal
intelligentsia that revived a culture that had been banned or partly
banned by the Soviets; it was they who set the tone in the media;
they who used innocuous-sounding, seemingly natural slogans to
lend their ideological support to the notorious reforms of the 1990s.

"Their will and their desire was directed, intentionally, at isola-
tion," the philosopher Alexander Pyatigorsky has said of this
intelligentsia.

This is how they thought about the government: "You are cretins, leave us alone—we will study higher math, theoretical physics, and semiotics. And everything will be fine." They failed to understand that in fact they were violating their own political conscience. They lacked the audacity and the will to recognize themselves as a political force. And when perestroika began, they were completely disorganized, intellectually, because they could not help but feel—instead of "they" I could say "we," it's merely a question of style—we could not help but feel that this very isolation, this very "leave us alone"—it was the same old "intelligentsia garbage." We need to formulate at least an approximate political ideal.[40]

The features ascribed to the liberal intelligentsia by Pyatigorsky surfaced in the late 1980s and early 1990s. It was then that all discussion of "socialism with a human face" was thrown overboard and a resurgent labor movement found itself under the heel of "democratic" reformists. This was the intelligentsia's first capitulation. The second began in October 1993, with their almost total acquiescence to the shelling of the Duma, and it ended in 1999 with Vladimir Putin's rise to power. During this time, in the context of a politics of complete capitalist restoration, a renunciation took place: not just of any oppositional attitude to the neoliberal model, but even of a more or less critical approach to it. (There were individual voices opposing this; they were drowned in the general chorus of loyalty.) The political opposition to Boris Yeltsin in the 1990s consisted largely of the Communist Party, a decrepit left-patriotic monster incapable of doing anything on its own, which nonetheless managed to become, for many years, a conduit for various moods of protest, even as it always performed the same exact ideological function: to be a scarecrow to the liberally minded elite. In this capacity it won Yeltsin a second term in office

40   The quote comes from an interview with Pyatigorsky published in the journal *Neprikosnovenny Zapas*, 2006, No. 3. The quote continues: "The one person who attempted to do this was Andrei Dmitrievich Sakharov. He was unable to do it, but for this you cannot blame him." Interview available at http://magazines. russ.ru/nz/2006/47/in5.html.

in 1996. A few years later, Putin was anointed king. At this point the liberal intelligentsia split psychologically and socially in two: one half became directly engaged in servicing the structures of capital—banks, publishing houses, corporations, and so on—while the other, less fortunate one, decided that regardless of all the hardships—the impossibility of working in one's field, the cultural degradation, the vulgarity and pettiness of the new overlords—it would be wrong to grumble, to express discontent, to make demands. It was futile and unattractive to go against the time. And then, early in this decade, came the rise of the national-patriotic "red-browns," who would be "even worse" than the current rulers, just as the Communists would have been "even worse" than Yeltsin. As a result, the two halves of the intelligentsia formed an ideal consensus. At that moment, any possibility for real opposition, real discussion, and real political life in Russia disappeared.

And now we've reached another turning point, because the red-brown scare is finally fading into the past. And a task that was wholly bungled at the beginning of the nineties is once again taking center stage: the creation of a real left-wing movement, based on workers' autonomy, on independent labor unions, on the cooperation of grassroots movements and organizations.

And how does the Russian intelligentsia confront this challenge? With another capitulation, its third in twenty years. Any discussion of capitalism is off limits. Capitalism is irrevocable. The younger generation, even in its best, most artistic, intellectual manifestation, already fights tenaciously for its right to a private life, to freedom from any talk of "politics," "ideology," or, even worse, the "proletariat." These words are associated with the beginning of the Nineties; today they seem hopelessly archaic, although in truth the political paralysis that destroyed Russia in the 1990s continues to this day.

\\\

An old liberal maxim still haunts the minds of the intelligentsia: it states that "everyone should mind his own business," including artists. This is a conception of the artist as a private citizen most lucidly articulated by Joseph Brodsky in his Nobel Prize address. Yet it is obvious that Brodsky himself, as a poet chosen and put forward by his own social circle, participated in certain bargains, had certain privileges, was published by certain houses, thus directly or indirectly supporting certain powers and ideologies. But poets like the idea of "purity," and one is supposed to acquiesce to the fiction that the poet is alone and that his texts, his political position (or its absence), and his personal qualities are in no way interrelated. And everyone should mind his or her own business—why meddle in someone else's private life? The person of letters should write, the politician should politic, the engineer should engineer, and so forth.

The idea that follows is that in a "normal" society, various strata would get along independently of one another: large corporations would be independent of the proletariat working in their mines and oil fields, bohemia would be independent of the large corporations whom it serves, and so forth. At the same time, nearly every person (especially every artist) wants to be considered unique, separate, independent, disconnected from conditions of, God forbid, "the relations of production." And the most important idea of all: that the current situation, whatever you wish to call it—"celebrity culture," "capitalism," "the Putin regime," and so forth—is total, that there is no escaping it. These ideas, which seem natural, but which date back to concrete historical conditions, explain the almost absolute hegemony of the "right" in Russian culture and politics today. These are a set of specific, deeply metaphysical ideas about the unshakable foundations of human nature. In their extreme-right, reactionary form, they are manifest in perceptions of the eternal characteristics of ethnic groups, races, nations; in their more or less liberal variant: of the irrevocable expansion of the market, which is impossible to wholly describe, to which one can only resign oneself, and within which the best one can do is find a tiny little niche.

It's as if, within this system, the artist were indulged as a vessel for a particular kind of political innocence: this is his social role.

The artist represents the idea of timeless, "apolitical" categories, of great masterpieces, of existential freedom. A poet is even freer than others, because unlike the artist, musician, or theater director, the poet doesn't need any capital to create works. The conditions of production are so cheap that a poet can believe his work is connected directly to the fabric of life, that it prevails over its context and circumstances. On an individual level this perception is perfectly reasonable and can be productive. In truth, the belief that your work can escape the stagnant social fabric is very important—it is a major stimulus to the production of art.

But when one idea comes to be shared by *all* poets, it begins to look suspicious. Right now, not only is the idea of the "private project" shared by all poets, it is also the rallying cry of artists, critics, and other intellectuals.

Some examples of the touching innocence that characterizes our leading cultural figures illustrate this: Vyacheslav Butusov, a former star of the punk underground, expresses genuine surprise that he should be criticized for performing at a rally for "Nashi," the Putin youth brigade; the fashionable theater director Kirill Serebrennikov criticizes the President in Aesopian language and is simultaneously the main guide of the Kremlin's cultural politics: he lectures under the aegis of the United Russia party.

The theater director Alexander Kalyagin signs a letter against the imprisoned Mikhail Khodorkovsky, in exchange for which he receives a theater in the center of Moscow, where he will, of course, stage his incorruptible oeuvres, where he will even stage Brecht—*ars longa, vita brevis!*

I recently found myself puzzled by one poet and critic who wrote a sympathetic article on "leftist poets" for a pro-Kremlin website[41]. He even expressed a kind of solidarity with the leftist

---

41   Igor Vishnevetsky. "Left Flank." *Vzglyad.* The website, Vzglyad.ru, was founded in 2005 by a young internet mogul named Konstantin Rykov, who is also known for his "For Putin!" and "Glory to Russia!" PR campaigns. The article

poets, cheerily urging them toward direct political action! And he did this not only from the right (it would not be notable if this were in the pages of the liberal journal *Znamya*), but from a space that was created by the Kremlin expressly to strengthen its power via the smokescreen of "parliamentary polyphony." When I wrote to say that I was surprised, he answered: "What difference does it make where the article is published; what matters is what is written in it"—again confirming my worst fears regarding the condition of the minds of even the most advanced and talented representatives of the intelligentsia.

What motivates these people is irrelevant: whether it's really political naïveté or just ordinary cynicism and prudence. It's impossible to separate one from the other, and I'm not posing a question of moral judgment. Russian culture as a whole has acquired (very much at the wrong time) the possibility of palpable autonomy, and now each individual artist sincerely defends his or her innocence and independence. But it is precisely through this kind of "innocence" and "sincerity" that works of art become commodities—not because the artist believes himself a spineless, prostituted insect, ready to do anything for publicity, but for exactly the opposite reason: because he values himself and his work very highly and believes that media appearances won't do him any harm.

\\\

Terms like "innocence" and "sincerity" frame the current mind-set to a remarkable degree. In all its dimensions—cultural, sociopolitical, and so on—the climate is determined not so much by "money" and "celebrity" (as is widely thought), but by the

---

in question, which is about Medvedev and the poet and critic Aleksandr Skidan, ends with the following paragraph: "Comrades Skidan and Medvedev (and I call them that without any irony, because I think that we believe in the same thing—Russian poetry—just with different methods)—don't you think it's time for us not only to decide which poetic or life style we should choose, but also to decide for direct action, overcoming individual style?"

"new sincerity." The new sincerity is President Putin and contemporary poetry and the broadcasters on television. It is Alexander Lukashenko admitting that his party falsified the elections—lowering Lukashenko's numbers from 93 percent to 80 percent—because, Lukashenko very sincerely confessed, "the European Union wouldn't have accepted the results otherwise." This is simultaneously unbelievable and symptomatic. The new sincerity is the blogosphere, with its absolutely sincere poets in one corner and its equally sincere Nazis in the other.

The "new sincerity" emerged in the culture as a reaction to the mind-bending abstractions of postmodern theory on the one hand and to a confused and conflicted (post-)Soviet consciousness on the other. There came a moment when direct expression—an appeal to biographical experience as a zone of authenticity—was the tool that could force open at least two discourses: the rough, ideologized Soviet one and the ascetic, bodiless, nonconformist underground one. Today, the trend toward "sincerity," "emotionalism," and "straightforward utterance," with its appeal to biography, has become more and more reactionary.

The new sincerity or, more precisely, the *new emotionalism*, has rejected the worst aspects of postmodernism: its unintelligible, elitist jargon and its opposition to grand narratives and global concepts. But it has also rejected its undeniably positive qualities: its irrepressible critical outlook and its intellectual sophistication. And if, in spite of its initial critical power, postmodernism in the end only gave cover to an idealized consensus between the goals of "diversity" and the interests of the global marketplace, then the new emotionalism reconciles those same market interests with the resurrected figure of the author, bringing forth today's endless stream of ventriloquism (lyrical, essayistic, "political," whatever), in which any effort at analysis, any possibility of differentiating positions and actions simply drowns. It's a stream in which it's impossible to separate sincerity from hack work, because one is in the employ of the other: emotions cover up ideological bankruptcy (and the death of rational argument), and ideology in turn excites emotions and captivates the masses. It's not hard to influence a person filled with emotions. The authorities are afraid of this sincerity, but they feed off and take advantage of it. Let young neo-Nazis scare the peasants with their sincere hatred, simultaneously keeping them in line. Let young poets and actors scream and curse from the stage of the Polytechnic: "Do whatever you want," the new commissars tell them. "You are free, independent artists. Just don't worry your pretty little heads about politics; after all, you're smart, you know yourselves that it's a dirty business. Your art will obviously outlive us all. Just leave the politics to us."

The new emotionalism never fully grasped the ambivalence of postmodern theory; now it rejects the idea of the death of the author and replaces the dead author with the uniquely living, all-consuming "I," granting it the right to say anything at all, whatever strikes its fancy. After all, if Marx is dead, everything is permitted. If "during postmodernism" language itself (as a system) spoke through the (dead) author, and embedded within this language were "schizophrenic" (liberating) possibilities, then in the new situation, when a long-repressed freedom of expression mingles with neoliberalism, it is God again who starts to speak through the poet. And this God is nothing but the rumblings, the convulsions, the subterfuges of capitalism itself, similar to ancient Fate, which all must inevitably confront, regardless of where they try to run.

Given this context, Russian poets' lamentations about their condition sound touchingly naïve. Why, they ask, don't we have normal literary criticism? I have a simple, vulgar answer to this question: because all the major critical theories of the West in the twentieth century passed, in one way or another, through Marxism. All took something from it, altered other things in it, invalidated something else. Until the same happens in Russia, there won't be any criticism at all—not of poetry, nor of the authorities.

\\\

In 1930, Bertolt Brecht ascribed the "humble nature of the political demands made by the avant-garde" to the fact that they believed, wrongly, that they were in charge of the mechanisms whereby their works were staged, published, and distributed. Six years later, Walter Benjamin produced an article called "The Work of Art in the Age of Mechanical Reproduction," in which, having also identified the process of capitalism's escalation into fascism, he mentions such concepts as "creativity and genius, eternal value and mystery—concepts whose uncontrolled (and at present almost uncontrollable) application would lead to a processing of data in the Fascist sense." Benjamin tried to introduce concepts that would be "completely useless for the purposes of Fascism." In "Charles Baudelaire," he showed to what extent the idea of an "absolute work" is transformed into an absolute commodity under the conditions of capitalism. Today, the "individual" project is just such a commodity. Indeed, the idea of an "absolute work" and the idea of an "individual," "biographic" project successfully complement each other. If within the art business, a biographical subtext is a necessary complement to the work-as-commodity, then in the media, on the other hand, an artist's work is a (sometimes unnecessary) surplus bonus atop his media image.

This situation presents leftist Russian art with a choice. In the 1990s, Moscow's leftist artists worked in conditions of a total absence of any legitimate leftist movement, so that no matter what one thought of any of them, they were still undeniably the carriers of the leftist tradition in its different forms. In the 2000s, some of them emigrated (Alexander Brener, Oleg Mavromatti, David Ter-Oganyan), while those who stayed in Russia (Dmitry Gutov, Anatoly Osmolovsky) chose the "path through the institutions": without renouncing their leftist ties, they nonetheless attached themselves to established galleries and official projects. Both have their justifications, perhaps; but the truth is that the individual voices of these artists merge with today's general loyal-apolitical background. We can hope that in the future their individual development will prove that they made the right choice, but as a whole we should admit that appeals by left-wing artists to pure art are usually a sure sign that one is living in an epoch of reaction. (One recalls Rodchenko, for whom the idea of a work's engagement with form in the '20s was replaced by the idea of pure form in the '30s, when engagement became official Stalinist doctrine.)

The author of the most brilliant individual project of the last few decades is Eduard Limonov. Throughout the 1990s and until quite recently, it was almost impossible to find a position from which a critique of Limonov would sound convincing. To take moral issue with him for excessive "sincerity" made you a hypocrite. To incriminate him as a "fascist" meant pretending that Yeltsin was a "democrat." Those who tried to belittle him or confront him with overt hostility were doomed to find themselves immediately in a system of coordinates created by the self-same Limonov, in which the critic invariably (by an aggregate of data: as a writer, as a politician, as a man) was found to be beneath the great poet. Limonov had charm and a heroic persona and a remarkable biography, but there was also something else in play—under conditions of the "individual project," any criticism is automatically followed with an answer from a position of experience: live my life (that is, visit as many cities and countries, write as many books, love as many women, create an equally independent and passionate political party), and then we'll talk. All of Limonov's heroes, even those more famous than he (Salvador Dali, for instance), eventually become just sad and transitory characters in the brilliant, vivid novel of Limonov's life.

Yet I think the era of Limonov's *cultural* hegemony (in which, undoubtedly, together with National Bolshevism and brown-red quasi-fascism, there were also progressive elements) is coming to an end. Today his political activity plays the reactionary role of subordinating all oppositional (and leftist) politics to Limonov's life project—his cult of personality, strategies of media-scandal, and so on. Leftist groups in Russia today work in the shadow of Limonov's NBP and its spectacular media events. With a cocktail made up of

Nietzscheanism, nationalism, and "leftism," mixed in with auto-biographical authenticity, Limonov has managed to subsume an important segment of the youth protest movement under his own banner.

Baudrillard believed that the revolution of '68 was defeated by overexposure in the media. The narrative of art-activism, the direct action of the '90s, has either led to the spectacular, partly fascistic activism of the NBP or to today's crossroads, where left artists choose between a job in the art market or a search for alternative strategies attempting to answer a question also faced by leftist political groups: how does one clothe the message in an adequate and legitimate form, simultaneously avoiding vulgar, spectacular excesses?

\\\

Today an artist who wishes to consider himself a leftist ends up trapped between these two positions. He wants to influence society, a fact he does not conceal, which is why he is skeptical in his approach to the concept of "pure art." On the other hand, he does not want to transmit himself directly through the media's mechanisms and needs to approach them carefully and critically.

For me, an important experience was a protest I staged against the Kalyagin theater during the premiere of Brecht's "Drums in the Night." It was conceived as a one-man protest (that is, a maximally democratic means of expression, accessible to all and with no pretense to artistic value or novelty) in a series of other protests organized by the socialist movement Vpered. It was interpreted, however, as an art action, partly because of a skirmish with the guard, partly because the reaction from right-liberal critics appealed almost exclusively to biography: Brecht's biography, my biography, the critic's biography. What one witnessed was a characteristically unthinking impulse: instead of a conversation about the enterprise as an effective or ineffective civil/political gesture, truthful or half-truthful or openly false facts from one's own or someone else's biography were pulled in. The critic would write, for example, that, in fact, "Brecht skillfully utilized capitalist mechanisms," or, in fact, "the protester has rich parents," or, "in my youth, I myself lived in a proletarian area, and I know what the proletariat is." OK.

I was born in 1975. My father was a journalist and a bibliophile. My mother worked as an editor at Soviet Writer, a publishing house. My father blossomed during perestroika. He conducted interviews with cultural figures in the magazine Ogoniok, *which was then widely read. In 1991, he and I went to "defend the White House [against the failed Communist putsch]." At the start of the nineties, he hosted a show about culture on television. To be honest, his blossoming did not last long. My father became addicted to roulette and soon lost everything: his real estate, our apartment, his library. He ran up a huge debt to the mafia. We lived in portable apartments, under constant threat. One time, I was taken as a hostage. In 1994, running from the mafia, my mother and I spent a month in Israel. Then we returned to Moscow. In Moscow I got a job as an ice cream vendor. (Once, I came to work the morning after my birthday. I had been drinking the night before and had lost my voice. All the customers thought that I had eaten too much ice cream. It was funny.) In addition to this, at the time, I also loaded trucks in a warehouse and worked as a book vendor. I remember the Moscow of those years through the eyes of a sleepless, almost homeless young man, a stranger to anything and everything. Sometimes I spent the night at home, more often with friends, but I basically lived on the streets because it was only on the streets—immersed in a crowd—that I felt free. Around me, on the one hand, there reigned an unhealthy, entrepreneurial chaos; on the other, poverty, hunger, cynicism, disintegration, and agony. Between 1992 and 1996, I studied history at Moscow State University. Between 1996 and 2000, I studied translation at the Gorky Literary Institute. During this period, I worked as a journalist and critic, wrote reviews and articles in newspapers and magazines, translated. Gradually I came to see that not only as a journalist, but even as a translator, I could not fit into this new reality, a fact I announced in the first line of my first intelligible poem, at the beginning of 2000. Now, from time*

to time, I do editing work, which is given to me by a publisher friend.
I live on money earned by my girlfriend. Until recently, this was $700
a month; now, after an exhausting battle, they raised her salary to
$1,100. The three of us—with our son, Bogdan—live on this money.
Recently I was thinking about the boundary between what I could and
couldn't afford, and I realized that if I take a pastry as an example,
then the boundary is around twenty rubles. Now, this does not depend
on an actual amount that I can spend during a single day, and it
does not depend on how much money is in my pocket. But psychologi-
cally, I'm left with this twenty-ruble pastry as the border between...
AHHHHHHH!!! What conclusions follow from these facts? Do
they have any meaning—these occasionally amusing, occasionally
incredible or tear-jerking facts? Do they justify or discredit my
position? Do they confirm one or the other of my grievances and
do they discredit the positions of others?

It's interesting to note that the use of gossip fits perfectly well
with stale declarations about the irrelevance of Marxism. And
somehow these kinds of facts are always accompanied by the fake
moralism that surfaces when certain media strategies are criticized
from a post-underground perspective—when people inevitably
start talking about "self-promotion" (the self-promotion of the
protester) in juxtaposition to "pure art." This position made a
certain amount of sense during the 1970s and early 1980s, when
working for a narrow, underground audience was actually a form of
political action. But today the autonomy of the artist, by which is
understood his freedom from any external ideology (he'll contemp-
tuously call this, appealing to the old categories, "the party line"),
is the central bulwark to the myth of the bourgeois artist and his
"individual project."

The artist is connected to his environment, stratum, and commu-
nity through a collective experience—bodily, historical, cultural.
In the artistic act, this connection manifests itself voluntarily,
which is why it is a moment of freedom. An artist can think,
reflect, and deduce as much as he wants outside the artistic act. But
only in the act of creation, only voluntarily, having become a kind

of blind, insane vessel, can one create a form—a form that connects a person with his biography, with his experience, with those unilluminated, chaotic, power-hungry clots in which his history joins up with the collective one. Only in this way can one break through to reality—to force someone to hate you or to express solidarity, to make someone think, to make someone experience collective oppression alongside you. This is why terms like "form," "sincerity," and "personal, biographical experience" are still, I think, significant even in politicized art, because manipulation either of one's own or of someone else's personal experience (as in art, so also in politics) ultimately leads to chaos, creating a deceptive unity—that is, yet another ideology or "individual project" in which even private or cultural experience only justifies powerlessness or conformism or a set of sentimental bromides. Please don't talk to me about your "historical experience" of Soviet oppression: it's not your experience, it's the experience of Mayakovsky (a Bolshevik), of Shalamov (a Trotskyist), of Mandelstam (a Socialist-Revolutionary), of others[42]. We must live our new, actual political experience, and if the goal of the "leftist" actionists of the 1990s consisted in bringing themselves and their bodies into the media's field of vision, then the goal of today's left artist must be to use one or another link to the outbursts of the oppressed and their underground movements—to discover his link to history, to those artists, philosophers, and fighters who have been cast aside or castrated in the contemporary "post-political" world.

Many of the twentieth century's "criticisms of cultural production" were based on the notion that through his stratum, class, or community, each person is connected with every other person, and having realized that his labor is expropriated and used against him and others like him, he can stop working, leave the game, and disrupt the machine. Conscious of the historical situation and, above all, intolerant of it, he can try to change that situation.

---

42   The poets Vladimir Mayakovsky, who committed suicide in 1930, and Osip Mandelstam, who died in a prison camp in 1940, and the poet and prose writer Varlam Shalamov, who spent almost twenty years in Stalin's Gulag, were all at some point leftists, as Medvedev points out.

In Russia right now, the intelligentsia's old default position—the "unextended hand," the supreme gesture of liberal impatience, based on the notion that any political/ideological opponent (in other words, a "Communo-fascist") was just a scoundrel (or, at best, crazy)—is falling further and further into disrepute. The new default position is a flaccid tolerance: Why make a choice at all? Why divide people into "reds," "whites," or what have you, if there's something familiar and interesting in everyone? Thus "postmodern sensitivity" lives on in the new era. In the face of private human feelings (love, loneliness, the fragility of relationships), any act of "debunking" or criticism resembles blasphemy. Don't ask the artist what he meant to say and whom he works for—he shouldn't think about that! What talk can there be about analysis or theory if it's a question of feelings—love, happiness, understanding—all so hard to attain in this world? How can you blame an artist for making people feel good? How can you blame a director who entertains people who are tired after a hard day's work? However false and deceptive the "national ideology," regardless of whose interests are behind it, what's wrong if it gives people at least an illusory feeling (but a feeling nonetheless) of confidence and community? Finally, can one blame "sovereign democracy"[43] if it alone allows us to retain a fragile balance, quieting real hypocrisy and thus avoiding even more serious catastrophes?

Taken to its extreme, it comes down to a single question that today hangs over our country and our world: What does it matter that a fraud took place if everyone's happy?!

But far from everyone is happy, and that means the final fraud hasn't happened yet.

---

43   Term coined by Putin ideologue Vladislav Surkov to describe Russian-style authoritarianism with elections.

\\\

In the Woody Allen film *Match Point*, a kind of remake of *Crime and Punishment*, the main character gets away with murder: he kills his mistress and an elderly neighbor who witnessed the crime. The detective on the case sees the truth, but only in his dreams. The murderer goes on with his life, and his wife finally gives birth to their long-awaited child.

With great clarity and subtlety, Allen compares Dostoevsky's era to our own. In Dostoevsky, madmen and grand inquisitors kill each other, but the world is ruled by a higher, divine justice that can only be deferred for so long before it reasserts itself with frightening force. However well everything goes for the criminal, sooner or later, truth, verity, and justice break the chain of accidents and enter the world, restoring balance; in Dostoevsky's Christian version, balance takes the form of a plea for forgiveness, not a punishment. The detective becomes a mediator of this higher, God-like fairness. In Woody Allen's postmodern world, there is no higher justice, only a game where everything depends on happenstance, on where the ball will fall (thus, "match point"). This sense of a fragile reality teetering on the edge is very prevalent in today's world and makes up what is called the "neoliberal" consciousness, with its—for the moment—almost complete political paralysis.

For the last few years, prophesies of an upcoming catastrophe have lingered in the Russian ether: the collapse of the country; all-out civil war; a foreign intervention; the appearance of a violent, repressive force. Many recent novels feature some form of violent shock. A characteristic example is Sergei Dorenko's *2008*, in which, in the midst of a triumphant, stable, and governable political landscape (there are three loyal forces in parliament: United Russia, "social democrats," and Zhirinovsky's Liberal Democratic Party), Chechen terrorists blow up a nuclear power plant outside Moscow, the capital empties, and Limonov and his cohort slide seamlessly into the Kremlin and establish a bizarre dictatorship. The consciousness of the writer reflects—fantastically and dismally—the myth of revenge that has haunted the minds of many Russian citizens since the 1990s. Translated into more or less intelligible terms, it sounds like this: For the past fifteen years, reality has been broken and stamped on; so many legal, moral, and human commandments have been violated; so many people were involved in so many hideous deeds (using their intellect, their power, their knowledge, or alternately their stupidity, their uselessness, their cynicism) that NOTHING GOOD CAN COME OF IT. And the longer the day of reckoning is delayed, the more terrible it will be when it arrives. That's why even today's relative happiness looks threatening. The authorities, the Kremlin, whoever, can postpone the inevitable with the help of oil money and a pliant media—but not forever. In this narrative (which is not all that far from the truth), the "fascists"—for example, Dorenko's Chechens—become a unique weapon of reckoning, of the restoration of justice. They suggest that you can use the people and lie to them as much as you want—but not forever. The truth will out, and it may be a lot worse than the lie. For today's loyal intelligentsia, these perceptions are channeled into yet another capitulation: let things remain as they are, they say, so long as we keep at bay the "red-browns," or the "fascists" (or Muslims, Chinese, and so forth).

Today, an alternative to both "wise" capitulationism and righteous, apocalyptic "retaliation" can only be a demand for "truth" in its totally concrete, everyday meaning—a fight for it, and for the formation of distinct political demands.

At the turn of the century, the mass anti-globalization protests in Seattle and Genoa, which wounded neoliberalism, as well as the attack on the World Trade Center, put an end to the cultural hegemony of the postmodern. Once again, a question was posed to capitalism, and a new era of critique began. At the same time a new reaction emerged—the conception of civilizational conflict, the axis of evil, and so forth. In this way, the opposition between metaphysics (the idea of "the eternal"—ethnic, national, confessional, civilizational values) and dialectics (the ideas of fluidity, interdependence, and the interchangeability of things) became relevant again.

\\\

There is a very heavy imprint of metaphysics on Russian life and thought. The metaphysical consciousness of the artistic intelligentsia is based, as I've said, on the idea that any product of nonmaterial labor exists outside its context and speaks for itself. Today, such ideas unite the majority of active politicians and successful artists, who have nothing against participating in official art projects, presuming that one can and should negotiate with the authorities. Of course you can try to fool them, taking their money and promoting something oppositional. These notions percolate in the consciousness of even very enlightened people, and, when added to the authorities' penchant for sponsoring fake oppositional political figures, they lead to the absence of real competition within the political field.

The opposite position argues that a civil society does not emerge from any "mutually beneficial" agreement with the authorities, even the most sympathetic authorities. It emerges only from the bottom, only as a call, a resistance, a demand. And culture also only emerges in this way.

You cannot criticize the Putin regime without assessing your own place in it, whether as critic or artist. You cannot criticize an authoritarian Russian democracy without also assessing the role of the United States and its allies, without mentioning the worldwide division of labor, without recognizing the extent to which the situation here is a continuation of worldwide processes. It's necessary to understand the extent to which your own consciousness determines your social existence, forces you to accept as obvious one or another set of perspectives. "There is no freedom from politics": this is the banal truth that one must now grasp anew. Political passivity also participates in history; it too is responsible.

The liberal intelligentsia, which has claimed for half a century that the subject of civil society is the quiet owner of his private life, is now confronted with a situation where the private life of the conformist and apolitical middle class is blooming in a previously unimagined array of colors in Russia while political life exists in a state of total nullity. All that's left here of the liberal-Western project is a rhetorical husk—complaints about "this country," our "bloody regime," and our forgotten "universal values." In truth, a total rejection of the 1990s unites practically the entire electorate, and those same liberal 1990s reforms (privatization, monetization of benefits, and so on) pass much more successfully under the banner of moderate patriotism and soft authoritarianism than under the slogan of inclusion in the "civilized world." Today, part of the intelligentsia shifts to the right, leaning toward ideas of a "clash of civilizations," trying to rely on "eternal"—national, ethnic, confessional, civilizational—values. Another part still insists that Russia has again turned from the path of civilized, Western capitalism.

\\\

The real need now is for the emergence of a new stratum of leftist intellectuals who have mastered the history of leftist thought, leftist politics, leftist art of the twentieth century and who have, through Western Marxism and neo-Marxism, recognized their participation in the international socialist project. This is, undoubtedly, the cultural and political goal of humanity—because it is precisely a participation in self-government on as broad a scale as possible— and not the possibility of a career, pure art, or a private life—that is that next step, without which humanity is doomed to moral and physical degeneration. The old slogan "socialism or barbarism" has become unbelievably relevant again. Because in order to keep open the possibility of remaining a private citizen, more victims will have to be brought forth; we will have to move further to the "right," become more embroiled in our individual projects, private territories, and narrow specializations demanded by the market. More protections once won by the Enlightenment and civil society will have to be sold to corporations, media conglomerates, and political marketing. We will have to fear the "radical" Chinese and Muslims more intensely and further insist on the totality of capitalism, the end of the working class, the end of class warfare, the end of politics (all concepts that envelop a person in a long, dreary sleep, in which he sees himself simultaneously a hero of cultural resistance, the last item up for sale, and an independent private person). Only roused from this sleep can a person realize what the world looks like shorn of any glamour, where again and again people who did not read Marx or Benjamin answer the call to resistance, to action, to an understanding of the shared interests of the collective, of the class. Whereas capitalism's violent reaction to every collective demand, every independent union, seems on the surface irrational, this violence is in fact completely logical and justified—because the front line is right here: the most narrow point where something happens that rarely occurs in poems, novels, or movies: a fight for reality. Only when we realize the reality of this battle will we be able to speak of separation, of individualism, of the possibility of genuine diversity, of a civil society, of a competition of ideas, forms, poetics. Only then can we believe in "apoliticism" and "privatism" as risky and culturally productive personal demands and not as banal projections of individualism, apathy, and lunacy. Only then will we be able to use the blogosphere, which undoubtedly possesses much progressive, even socialist potential, but which for now is a mechanism emerging directly from current conditions (which, we should notice, are entering back into it), meaning that in the best case it will be a way to spend some leisure time and in the worst it will become (like "direct democracy" as a whole) a weapon in the hands of the most ideologically active strata—neo-Nazis, for example.

I am convinced that without understanding the aforementioned things, the Russian intelligentsia too will remain, indirectly and directly, an agent of dark reaction.

"Literature Will Be Scrutinised" by Bertolt Brecht

Those who have been set on golden chairs to write
Will be questioned about those who
Wove their coats.
Not for their elevated thoughts
Will their books be scrutinised, but
Any casual phrase that suggests
Something about those who wove coats
Will be read with interest, for it may involve characteristics
Of famous ancestors.

Whole literatures
Couched in the choicest expressions
Will be examined for signs
That revolutionaries too lived where there was oppression.
Pleading appeals to immortal beings
Will prove that at the time mortals sat over other mortals.
The delicious music of words will only relate
That for many there was no food.[44]

---

44   English translation from: Bertolt Brecht, *Poems, 1913-1956*. John Willett and Ralph Mannheim, eds. Methuen. 1976. Page 344.

DMITRI PRIGOV [obituary]

Posted at zoltan-partosh.livejournal.com
July 16, 2007

For more on Prigov, see the glossary at the end of this book.

Translation by Keith Gessen

Dmitri Prigov (November 5, 1940 – July 16, 2007)

Prigov died today.

It's been a crazy summer. A transitional summer. Yesterday we watched *Cargo-200*[45]. It's a very timely film about the death of the Soviet Union. And the death of Prigov is also a death of the Soviet Union. "The death of the father," as Dmitry Kuzmin noted, rightly, on his blog. This is how I see it: We're transitioning, right now, to the era when the Soviet Union won't exist anymore. For twenty years we've been talking about how there's no Party anymore, no empire anymore, it's each man for himself, and so on. But this was a lie. Because the USSR still answered for everything, was still responsible for everything. For some, the Soviet Union was what they opposed: they were the new, free, entrepreneurial, Western Russians, unlike "them," the autistic, godforsaken, backward, totalitarian suckers. For others the Soviet Union was what they could exploit and appeal to—industrialization, the victory in the war, the first man in space, and so on.

Now both these discourses are dead, they have the same feeling of inner rot as Balabanov's film (even though he attacks the Soviet Union not from a liberal viewpoint but from his own Christian-nativist one). In this the current authorities have a kind of victory, as does the general "situation" (despite what Balabanov wants to say about it, which, as usual with his movies, isn't exactly clear). If we

---

45   A 2007 film by Alexei Balabanov (1959-2013), an accomplished mainstream post-Soviet film director. His films dealt in different ways with the violence, nihilism, and despair of the period after the Soviet collapse. His first film, *Brat* ("Brother"), was a *Taxi Driver*-like film about a traumatized young man returning from the war in Chechnya. Subsequent films dealt with the war more directly, as well as with drug addiction, prostitution, and the gang wars of the 1990s. *Cargo-200*, Balabanov's most shocking film, sets Faulkner's *Sanctuary* in a Soviet provincial town in 1984, at the violent, depressing tail end of the USSR, where no one is in charge anymore, but the coffins of young men (referred to as Cargo 200s by the military) continue to return from Afghanistan.

project this directly onto politics, we find that we are finally witnessing the collapse of the ultimately pretty inglorious 15-year history of the Communist opposition. By the same token this should be the end of the pathetic failure that is the so-called "democratic" opposition and its equally constant, and equally helpless, appeals to the figure of the father, the Soviet Union. "They're forcing us back to the USSR!" cry the liberals, "This is exactly how they did it in the Soviet Union," and so on. Bullshit. No one's forcing anyone back to the USSR; everything's different now. Just as there's almost *nothing* in *Cargo-200* about the present day, even though there are a lot of apparent historical coincidences: the awful police, the cowardly conformist intelligentsia, and so on. But you can sense that things are different.

The new epoch we're finally entering, the epoch without a USSR, is defined by the fact that the USSR can no longer help anyone. You can no longer use it positively or negatively—you just can't. The only thing to do now is *live without it*.

Now, a few words on Prigov. First of all, Prigov was, in my opinion, one of the great postwar poets: Prigov; Brodsky; Vysotsky[46]. These are three genuine, immortal faces of the anti-Soviet discourse—the intellectual-critical, the intelligentsia, and the democratic. These are the "figures of the father" in whose shadow everything took place over the last thirty years. Prigov was the last of them. There were many arguments around Prigov. For some he was the soulless product of mechanical conceptualist evil, in response to which it felt so good to be a divinely inspired poet! For others he was a symbol of the fact that for all the pathos, heartache, historical searching of his poems, one could in the end just relax and receive "pleasure" (or torture) from the "text." For a third kind of reader or writer (the "post-conceptualist" kind), Prigov was the one figure you needed to overcome and push away. But, any way you looked at it, he was a father. And just as we now

---

46   Vladimir Vysotsky (1938-1980). Popular and beloved Soviet film and stage actor, poet, and singer (in the Russian "bard" tradition).

consider arguments about whether or not Brodsky and Vysotsky were "good" poets absurd, so too it no longer matters whether Prigov was good or bad, but only how we'll live and form ourselves and our world *without* Prigov, just as we must now do without the Soviet Union.

I remember a poem of his, kind of a patriotic one in fact, and just apropos in general, I think.

> Young people—they come to me for advice.
> What can I say?
> Study, study, study! But they've been told that already.
> Get married? They'll get married without me.
> Marrying and studying—
> That's everyone's lot.
> Maybe I'll say to youth, all demon-like,
> Live where living is impossible:
> Now that's life!

IN PRAISE OF EVOLUTION [poem]

Published at Vpered.org.ru
July 3, 2007

Translation by Keith Gessen

The owner of a factory—underworld nickname: Toothache—sat in a cafe wondering how he was going to break the labor union.

For a while this was the most important thing in his life.

He was developing some ideas about it when all of a sudden a group of comrades walked past the cafe bearing a red flag.

The factory owner decided that the revolution had come and he began to repent, and shed tears, and share his profits with the workers.

But it turned out the parade was part of a slow evolution, and there was still plenty of time to exploit, crush, and kill.

AN INVITATION

[action]

Posted at zoltan-partosh.livejournal.com
November 21, 2007

Translation by Keith Gessen

I just received the following e-mail:

Tuesday, November 27, 7 PM

Guelman's Gallery at VinZavod

*Marat Guelman—Miroslav Nemirov—Konstantin Krylov
and the Crazy Madmen Who Are Crazy Again Collective*

Konstantin Krylov in all his manifestations—poet Yurik
Sherman, sci-fi writer Mikhail Kharitonov, historian of phi-
losophy False-Diogenes Pseudo-Laertsky, political thinker
K. Krylov, editor-in-chief of the news portal Agency of
Political News, founder of the Russian National Movement,
organizer of the Russian Marches.

Poems, prose, possibly songs.[47]

If this was sent just to make me angry, it didn't work. I'm already
angry. Then again, it probably wasn't sent to make me angry. It was
sent to invite me to come watch this unnatural coupling of art-
business-politics, a counter-culture that has lost its mind, and the
intellectual representatives of Nazism. Then again, why unnatural?
It's perfectly natural. Right? FUCK OFF.

(I'm turning the comments off on this post, just in case some
friends of mine to whom this kind of pornography is not alien will
try to explain to me why it's important to separate the text from its
author, aesthetics from ideology, and not raise such a ruckus about
minor things, etc. And after all I'm always happy to discuss things.
But here there's nothing to discuss.)

---

47   Marat Guelman is a fashionable gallery director whose "Russia 2" exhibit
Medvedev had protested in 2005; Konstantin Krylov is a young nationalist writer
and thinker. The Russian March is an annual march of nationalists, some of them
outright fascists, that began in 2005.

STANISLAV MARKELOV [obituary]

In the years from 2008 to 2011, much of Medvedev's energy went into party work for Vpered and the growth of the Free Marxist Press. Medvedev edited Vpered's lively website (Vpered.org.ru) and contributed numerous commentaries on political and other events. He also organized and participated in protests against the Putin regime—against its support for fascism; its support of the Moscow-Petersburg highway meant to cut through the Khimki forest north of Moscow; of the Unified State Examination, a standardized test for high school students first introduced in 2001 but made national and mandatory in 2009.

In these years, the battle against Russian fascism had heated up on the streets, as several activists from the antifascist organization Antifa were murdered. On January 19, 2009, the antifascist lawyer Stanislav Markelov was murdered by gunshot in Moscow in the middle of the day by a member of a Nazi organization.

Posted at Vpered.org.ru and zoltan-partosh.livejournal.com
January 19, 2009

Translation by Keith Gessen

Stanislav Markelov (May 20, 1974 – January 19, 2009)

This afternoon Stanislav Markelov was killed in the center of Moscow. Anastasia Barburova, a journalist from *Novaya Gazeta* who was with Markelov and tried to detain the person who shot him, died this evening from her wounds.

Everyone who follows the news knows of Markelov as the lawyer for the Kungaev family, whose daughter was raped and murdered by Colonel Yuri Budanov in Chechnya. Stas was indeed the lawyer in many well-known cases—the Nord-Ost terrorist attack, the attack on the journalist Mikhail Beketov, the murder of the anti-fascists Alexander Rokhin and Fedor Filatov. But Markelov also took on many more cases that are less well-known—of migrant workers murdered by Nazis, young army draftees attacked by their seniors, and residents protesting against the nearby construction of a nuclear power plant. Markelov is well-known to independent labor activists, whom he advised many times in their conflicts with employers and the authorities.

We can only speculate as to who is responsible for this murder—Nazis, ex-soldiers, the authorities. In any case, we can say for certain that what happened today is not just the murder of a human rights activist and antifascist, but a crime AGAINST JUSTICE. All of Stas's activity, all his energy and knowledge, was directed in the fight against injustice and in defense of those who suffer every day at the hands of the authorities, of capital and its mongrels.

The continuation of this battle will serve as the best memorial to him.

ATTACK ON CITY HALL
[poems]

Medvedev's Free Marxist Press stepped up its activity radically
in 2009 and 2010, publishing among other things a translation
of Terry Eagleton's *Marxism and Literary Criticism*, translated
by Medvedev; Herbert Marcuse's "Why I'm a Communist" (also
translated by Medvedev); and a collection of essays, *Bolshevism
and the 21st Century*, by the French Trotskyist Daniel Bensaïd.

In mid-2010, Medvedev opened a personal Facebook account.
In 2011, in the wake of the Arab Spring and renewed hope for
Russian radicals, he began posting some poems there.

Posted periodically on the author's Facebook page
www.facebook.com/kirill.medvedev.7
2011–2012

Translation by Keith Gessen

they said we could have an antifascist meeting, but not a march.
the human rights activist Lev Ponomarev[48] and I went to City Hall
to find out what was up.
Ponomarev was very angry. I tried to restrain him.
"I'll teach them to let the fascists march," he said.
You got the feeling this wasn't going to end well.

The deputy head of the department for large demonstrations,
   Vasily Oleynik,
turned out to be a fat rosy little man.

"You see," he began, smiling, "the decision on this matter has
   already been made."
"Do you know Russian?" Ponomarev asked grimly.
"But we're speaking Russian right now!" said Oleynik.
"No. If that's how you begin a conversation, then you don't know
   Russian,"
said Ponomarev.

That's how it began, with a little light antagonism,
but then it seemed to improve.
There was smiling, and diplomacy.
"But of course you understand, Lev Alexandrovich."
"Yes of course, Vasily Vasilievich."

"We already told everyone about the march," I said grimly.

---

48   Lev Alexandrovich Ponomarev (1941–). A physics professor during Soviet
times, Ponomarev was one of the founders of the human rights group "Memorial"
in the late 1980s. He was a comrade of Andrei Sakharov and in the 1990s a
member of parliament. In the last decade he has been an active member of the
opposition to Putin. In March 2009 he was attacked and beaten outside his home
in Moscow. His activity since then has only accelerated.

"There's no going back." Oleynik began citing legalities.
Pono gave as good as he got
in that department,
and my attention wandered a little.
Once they start in with the clauses and sub-clauses and anti-clauses,
everything turns into a joke, a scam, like in court
(and I don't like these kinds of scams).
Outside, I could see the river.
I recalled how, on October 2, 1993, the night before the opposition
stormed City Hall[49],
the cops took a group of us in
for supposedly breaking a window at the self-same City Hall.
At the precinct I argued very convincingly
that we hadn't broken any windows,
and the cops let us go.
Later on it turned out that the window had been broken by me,
but I'd forgotten.
Oh holy drunkenness!
How easy and pleasant it is to lie!
Have you heard how jackals cry?
Now, in City Hall, I remember the cry of some jackals in an
    Abkhazian village.
It's not even a cry,
It's like some wedding party has spilled out into the street.
Spills out and yells and sings and sings aloud!
in that village the people feared an invasion of raccoons, from the north,
from the Russian border.

---

49   In September 1993, Boris Yeltsin announced the recalcitrant parliament, the Supreme Soviet, dissolved. The leaders of the opposition refused to go, however, and called on their supporters to take up arms. In early October, armed supporters entered the parliament, stormed and took over City Hall (which is nearby), and then marched on the Ostankino television tower, where they were turned back after a bloody engagement. Subsequently, the army shelled the parliament and flushed out the opposition. Estimates of the number dead range from two hundred to two thousand.

I was startled from these thoughts by noises in the office—
a crunching, running, turning over of chairs—
my worst fears had materialized—
Ponomarev was beating the shit out of Oleynik!

I started running around him, crying,
"Lev Alexandrovich, no, don't,
oy, please don't, why?"

Through my protestations you could hear
Oleynik, moaning,
then he stopped moaning, because I started thinking,
and it was as if the sound
had been turned off, leaving only the picture, which unspooled in
    slow motion.

Nor could I hear what Ponomarev was saying.
But what can a person say who's proudly defending
his rights?
But he was talking:
"I know you, you spoiled little socialists,
unable to defend yourselves or others.
Quasi-sectarians, children,
ignorant of your rights.
Little marginal whiners.
Old maids from the library.
Are you a subculture or a political party—
make up your minds—
what are you?"

Oleynik's boss, Kadatsky, didn't come
to the aid of his deputy. He was at a meeting.
He'd sent Oleynik to meet with us
but didn't come to help him, just stayed at the meeting.
Coward.

A sense of one's rights gives a person physical force,
I thought, watching as Pono smashed up Oleynik.
Whereas we, on the left, never really feel our rights,
just the ephemeral right to utopia.
All those years of discussing the victims of the revolution
have frozen our blood,
have turned us into
frightened ducklings, unable to defend our own rights,
much less someone else's,
thought I, already out into the street,
out of that hell,
riding the subway home late in the evening.
And I'd have kept thinking this way,
for quite a while,
except then I got an email from Ponomarev:
They still hadn't allowed the march.
Tomorrow we head again for City Hall.

\\\

On the way to defend the forest[50]
I thought about powerlessness.
In my mind I turned over the old thought about how
the use of weapons is the sign of powerlessness.
That's what I was thinking about
when a division of the OMON riot police started coming toward
    us, and everyone freaked out, not from a philosophical but from a
    very earthly and real feeling of powerlessness.
I giddily recalled a line from some anarchist manifesto
about how only those who have weapons
are able to philosophize about pacifism.
if they just gave us some weapons, I thought, we could do some
    great philosophizing about pacifism.
And then suddenly from this apex of our powerlessness a weapon
    appeared:

We parted and from out of this mass of student-pacifists,
useless intellectuals and local pensioners,
a machine gun started firing.
The OMON troops started falling
like the trees of the Khimki forest.
"But the main thing is for there to be no revolution," said the
    environmentalist Evgenia Chirikova
as we stood over the bloody troops of the riot police wondering what
    to do next.
"There were fewer people killed during the October Revolution
than there were today," I said.
"But then consider how many people were killed during the civil war,"
said Mikhail, next to me.

---

50   In the summer of 2010, many Russian activists, including Medvedev,
became involved in an attempt to keep the government from running the new
Moscow-Petersburg highway through the heart of the Khimki forest north of
Moscow.

"That's because the army and the police didn't come over to the
    side of the people,'"
said someone else nearby,
and then we drank a little vodka,
we all drank for the police and the army
to come over to the side of the people,
that is to say our side,
and at that moment we saw on the highway,
dressed up as OMON fighters
in camouflage suits the color of the forest,
our reinforcements were on their way.

\\\

if you're having some problems, or feeling sad, I recommend you
    take a weekend evening
and go with a group of antifascists to Myasnitskaya Street, next to
    the Moo-Moo Cafe,
and while hearing people honking in the distance start heading for
    the center,
reach the beautiful empty square at Lubyanka,
pass by the FSB thinking about
how one day we'll pass by this rotten citadel
in such a way that *nothing*
will be left of it,
round the corner and find,
to your surprise, that the guards at Lubyanka aren't reacting at all,
are even, it seems, showing you respect,
reach Kuznetsky Most while shouting "Freedom to Denis
    Solopov!"[51]
and
"Don't stop antifa!"
sense with a light euphoria that today the center is ours,
watch as a comrade turns over a metal barricade next to the
    entrance to the FSB,
watch as he's attacked by a policeman, watch as those near him
    pull the policeman off, keep walking down Kuznetsky,
wonder why everyone seems so relaxed
today, reach Tverskaya, all thirty of you,
and block one half of it to traffic before, finally sensing a cop car
    behind you,
scattering next to Okhotny Ryad,

---

51   Denis Solopov (1987–). An antifascist activist who was accused of vandal-
izing the town administrative headquarters at Khimki in the summer of 2010.
Solopov fled Russia for Ukraine after his bother Maxim was arrested in Moscow.
He was detained by Ukrainian authorities, then released, and was given political
refugee status in Holland.

keep in mind that this is not in the end a panacea,
it's not even really medicine,
this is a political act and nothing more,
so if you have a problem then after a while
you'll still have to figure out how to solve your problem,
but antidepressants won't help anymore, psychotherapy
won't help, books and CDs won't help, nothing that you bury your
    lives into
thinking that this is the sad but only possible fate for a
free human being
will help.

UDP subscriptions are available on a rolling basis. All levels include a 15% discount on books, seminars, and swag, plus invites to special events.

- full presse subscription: $240 or $20/month
  a package every season (4 packages, 20+ titles)
- half presse subscription: $144 or $12/month
  a package every other season (2 packages, 10+ titles)
- membership: $60 or $5/month
  includes a bundle of books and a tote bag
- chapbook subscription: $60 or $5/month
  all chapbooks (2 to 3 packages, 7+ chapbook titles)

For higher level bibliophile and collector subscriptions see our website: www.uglyducklingpresse.org/subscribe

UDP is a 501(c)(3) nonprofit and registered charity. Donations are tax-deductible. Please consider a one-time gift or recurring support.

Keeping poetry ugly since 1993.

Who needs poetry.

This year, Ugly Duckling Presse is celebrating 25 years of publishing poetry, translation, experimental nonfiction, performance texts, and books by artists. Help keep the presses running by becoming a member or subscriber.

www.uglyducklingpresse.org/subscribe
www.uglyducklingpresse.org/donate

\\\

The wife of an activist who died under strange circumstances,
though more likely than not it was an accident,
says to me that she literally finds herself shaking
from everything that's going on, the arrests and the interrogations
    of activists...
I'm sure you know the story of N, she says.
A labor activist, they planted drugs on him, he got five years.
International campaigns have proved useless.
Yes, I said, I know, of course.
So what can we do, she says, what sort of action can we plan,
so that everyone finds out? What should we do?
And I say, we have two choices. Either we patiently build the
labor unions ... or we have to do something really ugly,
because no radical art actions are going to help here,
are going to get through.
And she says, yes, and then what? We commit a terrorist act? That's
    the same thing
right now
as sticking your head out of the trench,
and getting it blown off...
And as for labor unions, she says,
I know the labor activists,
they're wonderful people, but
it's all
so slow...
How long will it take,
although, it's true, it's the only way.
in the end it's the labor unions
that are the true workshop of communism.
Yes, I say, right now that's the situation,
no matter what anyone says,
and who knows what the future may bring, but for the moment
the progressive labor activists have a higher political consciousness

than the intellectuals,
than the professors,
it's just too bad there are so few of them.
But strategically that's the most important thing.
She says, You're right, I'm disappointed I wasn't able to unionize
the train conductors,
they're too attached to their private interests…
Night comes on
the cold streams in, streams in, streams in,
and enters
through the gates, through our sleeves
through our skin
enters our blood,
and somewhere in a warm room
on a soft bed on white
sheets
a pretty young mother
is stroking her little child
sleep sleep sleep my little one
sleep my baby child
sleep sleep don't listen
to the wind howling
the cars rustling
sleep tighter my little one
gather strength
you'll need lots of strength
the working class needs brave strong tough fighters
there are difficult times ahead.

COMRADE KOTS

(poem)

Medvedev was an active participant in the anti-Putin protests of late 2011 and early 2012, often appearing with his band, Arkady Kots. As activists began getting arrested around Moscow, agents taking smoke breaks outside the FSB building started hailing Medvedev as "Comrade Kots" when he walked by.

Published on Facebook
March 11, 2013

Translation by Keith Gessen

You say to me: Baby, I'm so worried
You're going to get mixed up in the arrests
For the goddamn May 6 protest[52].

I say, Look, we're already in the fire.
There's nothing else for us to fear.
You're registerghed on Little Kiselny Street,
We live together on Lower Kiselny Street,
We live in the center of Moscow,
Alongside blocks and blocks of FSB:
The old Cheka basements, the torture chambers,
The millions, the billions of ruined lives.

Oh, it's a nice system the Bolsheviks invented.
My comrades, my intellectual forebears.
Now it's run by their distant heirs,
Not iron-willed masters, but pathetic losers:
Shady characters with forgettable faces.
Though not so dumb, when it comes down to it.
And we're living here with them in this communal apartment.
When they see me on the street they call my name as if they own it:

Comrade Kots, how's it going?
Comrade Kots, where you going?
Comrade Kots, why not come in,
Comrade Kots, Comrade Kots,
Comrade, Comrade, Comrade
Kots.

I say: Don't worry, they haven't got a thing on me, nothing.
Remember: that was the night we went out dancing.

---

52   The largest of the anti-Putin protests took place at Bolotnaya Square in
Moscow on May 6, 2012. It was the last of the big protests. In its wake dozens of
activists have been arrested and imprisoned on charges related to "Bolotnaya."

Then again, you saw it on Channel One and the newspapers said
That I gave one of those cops a kick to his motherfucking head.

But still, I don't think they take marginal people like me.
The whole intelligentsia will rise up to defend me.
The human rights activists and the EU Parliament,
The Estonian Union of Writers, and the Italian Communists.

You see, that's why they're afraid of me,
I don't know why you're laughing.
I can't understand why you're crying.
Everything's fine, everything's great, I'm free.
We're sitting in the kitchen, and it's almost spring outside.
Though all around us, blocks and blocks of FSB…

Comrade Kots, how's it going?
Comrade Kots, where you going?
Comrade Kots, why not come in,
Comrade Kots, Comrade Kots,
Comrade, Comrade, Comrade
Kots.

LIBYA IS SERBIA [poems]

In winter of 2013-14, a mass protest movement in Ukraine over-
threw its president, Viktor Yanukovych. Medvedev and his friends
in Moscow had been watching events carefully, with excitement
and also wariness. On the one hand they were witnessing a revolu-
tion against a nasty regime; on the other hand the revolution was
taking place under the banner of neoliberal politics and right-wing
nationalist symbology. Whatever you thought of the result, its sig-
nificance could not be denied. "For the second time in ten years,"
Medvedev wrote at OpenLeft.ru, a new leftist website, "Ukraine
has revolutionized the minds of the Russian intelligentsia." Over
the course of the next year, as Russia first annexed Crimea and
then sent military equipment and personnel into eastern Ukraine,
Medvedev repeatedly spoke out against the Russian invasion, even
as he continued to be skeptical of the new regime in Kyiv and its
many oligarchic and right-wing friends.

Published on Facebook
Summer 2014

Translations by Keith Gessen

Volunteer

It's just I didn't have very much doing
it's just they weren't paying my salary
it's just I really wanted adventure
it's just the homeland was in danger.

I left behind my wife and my daughter:
this I remember clearly.
We walked through hills and forests.
It was like the summer camp I attended yearly.

Sometimes we shot at our own.
(Sometimes you shot at your own.)
Sometimes we called for peace.
We had a gray-brown-and-white ribbon.

In the black-white-and-brown silence
in the dark-brown-and-brownish silence
I put a swastika on my lapel.
People in black destroyed my body

they ripped the swastika off me
there's a hole in the spot where my heart was
a piece of shrapnel tore through me.
It must have been the Chechens who did it to me.

Libya is Serbia

Down with false peacemaking
say the backseat political analysts.
"Yes yes," says a man who's lost his hearing from the shelling.

Look, it's your daughter, she's in Syria now,
she's sick. But it'll be ok.
And we'll seek vengeance.
Because Libya is Serbia.

And you yourself are sick,
and you're not going to get better, my friend,
because progress is inexorable.
That is, no matter how much you try to exorcise it
it won't reach you anyway.

Because you're pining for the past, my friend,
pining for the past.
You're pining for the past,
which is free only in a mouse trap.

You should look around instead,
at the sea, the wind, the wheat.
Look at the stars,
the girls, all the beauty.

Look at me, your television host,
and understand once and for all that peace is impossible.

Facebook

It's only on Facebook that everything is great for me
good photos from beautiful places
interesting thoughts, journeys, respect from my many "friends"
any American university would accept me
but in real life everything's different:
just an unstructured waste
the same cafes again and again
my dad and mom always bugging me
turned out I couldn't afford my own place
my intellectual labor isn't protected
intellectual property isn't protected
the men I meet are boys, they're not attractive but they are aggressive
I know some nice ones, but even then I'm unsatisfied
and somehow I feel like it's my fault
and to hell with it, really, but here as with everything
you feel you have to confront the endless resistance of shit,
the endless resistance of shit.
That's how it is offline. But you wouldn't know it from my
    Facebook, right?
I've always been able to talk about things like this without shame
but it's bad manners to be whining all the time.[53]

---

53   A reference in part to the "heavenly hundred," the men and women who
died on Maidan during the anti-government protests in Kyiv early in 2014.

GLOSSARY OF NAMES

Alexander Brener (1957–). Poet, writer, and art-activist. Born in Almaty, Kazakhstan, studied in Leningrad, moved to Israel in 1989, returned to Moscow in 1992 where, along with Oleg Kulik and Andrei Ter-Oganyan, he became one of the founders of Moscow Actionism. This movement focused on provocative public actions as its art works. When, in 1994, Kulik performed his first action as a mad naked dog guarding the sanctity of the art world (he was in fact guarding the gallery of his gallerist, Marat Guelman), Brener held the leash. In 1995, not long after the start of the first Chechen War, Brener went out into Red Square in boxing shorts and boxing gloves and challenged President Boris Yeltsin to a boxing match (if Yeltsin wanted to fight, he should fight Brener), shouting: "Yeltsin! Come here! Yeltsin! Come here!" Another time, Brener got to his knees and shit his pants (or pretended to) in front of a Van Gogh in the Pushkin Museum of Art while repeating "Vincent" over and over (as a sign of his prostration and helplessness before Great Art). In 1997, in the most internationally well-known action of Moscow Actionism, he spray-painted a green dollar sign on Malevich's painting *Suprematisme 1920-1927* in an Amsterdam museum, an action for which he served five months in an Amsterdam jail. While in jail he wrote a book. He now resides abroad, in Vienna, and has published numerous books of poetry and political provocation. (Kulik remained in Moscow and became the most famous of the Moscow Actionism group. He later hosted in his studio the meetings of the Voina ["War"] art group, from which the punk group Pussy Riot would emerge.)

Joseph Brodsky (1940–1996). Born in Leningrad, Brodsky made the uncharacteristic decision, for a Soviet child of the intelligentsia, to drop out of middle school and start working—first at a factory, then at various other odd jobs, including janitorial work at a morgue. He began writing poetry in his mid-teens and was quickly acknowledged among his peers as a prodigy. He joined the nascent Leningrad quasi-underground scene in the late 1950s; his poems, inspired improvisations in a classical mode, circulated in some of the first samizdat anthologies. In 1964 he was arrested for "parasitism," or loitering, in part because he did not have a job and was unconnected to any institutions of Soviet life. His behavior during the trial that followed was exemplary; the transcript of the proceedings, taken surreptitiously by a brave woman named Frida Vigdorova and subsequently published in samizdat and in the West, made Brodsky world-famous for his insistence on his dignity as a poet and his right to be left alone. He was sentenced to five years' labor in the North, though released after two. In 1972, he was exiled from the Soviet Union. His first act in the West was to pay a visit to W. H. Auden outside Vienna. Eventually he settled in New York, where he continued to write poetry and also began contributing essays to the *New York Review of Books*. He won the Nobel Prize for Literature in 1987, and became the American Poet Laureate in 1991.

Dmitry Bykov (1967–). The most prolific and chameleon-like writer of his generation, Bykov, who began as a poet and high school teacher, has as of 2012 published ten collections of poetry, six novels, four story collections, and three full-length biographies of major Soviet figures (Boris Pasternak, Maxim Gorky, and Bulat Okudzhava). He is also a regular columnist in several newspapers, from the oppositionist *Novaya Gazeta* to the business magazine *Profil*, as well as a television personality—he was the founder and host of the popular (and very funny) NTV show *Vremechko*, which was, throughout the 1990s, a half-hour quasi-satirical news program. His poetry is nostalgic, his novels are satiric, and his biographies are polemical. An ordinary urban liberal in the 1990s, early in the Putin era he joined a number of intellectuals in denouncing the excesses of that decade. In 2003, he became a writer for a new, nationalist newspaper called *Konservator* ("The Conservative"); in 2007, he became a writer for the anti-liberal magazine *Russkaya Zhizn'*. But Bykov is nothing if not adaptable, and also very talented. In the wake of the fraudulent Duma elections, he has emerged as a leading and energetic figure in the movement opposing the continued rule of Putin and United Russia.

Dmitry Kuzmin (1968–). A poet, critic, and publisher in Moscow who has headed up an astonishing number of projects, publications, and initiatives, both in print and online. In 1989 he founded a young poets' group called Vavilon ("Babylon"), which in 1991 hosted "the first and only all-Soviet festival of youth poetry" and in 1992 started publishing books under the Library of Young Writers series. In 1993 Kuzmin founded a publishing house called ARGO-RISK (among other things, it published Medvedev's second book, *Incursion*, in 2002). The stated goal of the project from the start was to provide a space for young writers whom no one wanted to publish because the market was then flooded with all the books that had been banned or suppressed during the Soviet era. Kuzmin published an annual print anthology of young poetry called *Vavilon*, which also started publishing online in 1997. In 1996 he founded an anthology of Russian gay writing called *Risk*. From 1996 to 2002 he edited *Literary Life of Moscow*, a paper that described all the literary events taking place in the capital (and at which Medvedev worked). From 2000 to 2004 he ran a club called Avtornik, which hosted many readings. In 2004 he founded a new literary journal called *Vozdukh*. Online, *Vavilon* hosts an exhaustive catalog of Russian poets, with a large selection of their texts, biographies and photos, as well as literary "maps" and reviews of Russian poetry.

Eduard Limonov (1943–). One of the most compelling and contradictory figures of post-Soviet life, Limonov was a talented poet and beatnik who came to Moscow from his native Kharkov (Ukraine) in the early 1970s; he was soon kicked out of the country, ending up in New York, where he refused to become a professional anti-Soviet personage and instead produced a profane quasi-memoir, *It's Me, Eddie*, about the life of an impoverished immigrant trying to survive in the big city. After the Soviet Union fell, Limonov returned to Russia and quickly became involved in politics, forming the National Bolshevik Party (NBP) with the philosopher-provocateur Alexander Dugin in 1992. The party was at least quasi-fascist in both its political platform—which lamented the loss of the Soviet republics and called for the return of a Russian empire—and its regalia: its flag was a striking black hammer and sickle inside a white circle on a red background, which ended up looking a lot like the flag of the German Nazi Party. At the same time, in its early years the party under Limonov's direction was in many ways more of an art-action than a genuine political group: Limonov one time convened a press conference, declared that he was going to clean up the NBP, and proceeded to give one of the party's young members a haircut. It also published a very lively newspaper, *Limonka* (both a play on Limonov's name and Russian slang for a hand grenade). Limonov himself continued to produce books—mostly memoirs, but since these described his life in politics they were also political declarations and analyses.

In the 1990s, the mostly teenage members of NBP mostly confined themselves to throwing vegetables at visiting foreign dignitaries. As time wore on, things became more serious. In 2001, Limonov and another NBP member were arrested and accused of weapons smuggling, allegedly as part of a plan to invade Northern Kazakhstan (whose population is mostly ethnic Russian) and declare a Russian republic. Limonov spent two years in prison. When he got out in 2003, the NBP, while still very small, became the lone oppositional force in Russia willing to take to the streets. In their political statements they downplayed their old nationalism and instead focused on a fierce and consistent (and courageous) anti-Putinism. There were frequent arrests; the creation, by the Kremlin, of youth groups (first Walking Together, then Nashi) to compete with the NBP; and increased attention to Limonov. In spring of 2007 the NBP aligned with oppositional liberals to organize the March of the Dissenters, which became for the next several years the major outlet for opposition to the Putin regime. In the most recent protests, Limonov has found himself sidelined by events, unwilling to participate except on his own terms. In 2014, he came out in support of the Russian annexation of Crimea.

Dmitri Aleksandrovich Prigov (1940–2007). Radical poet, founder of Moscow Conceptualism along with Ilya Kabakov, Lev Rubinstein, and others. Prigov's poetry was a mixture of European poststructuralism and wry late-Soviet humor ("part Derrida, part Monty Python," as one American observer aptly put it). After the fall of the Soviet Union he emerged as the most active member of the Conceptualist generation, and therefore the flashpoint for arguments about whether Conceptualism represented a valid poetics. For some die-hards he was also a "mainstreaming" figure, who took Conceptualism public when really it ought to have remained underground.